Steck Vaughn

Target Spelling 1260

Margaret Scarborough
Mary F. Brigham
Teresa A. Miller

Harcourt Achieve

Rigby • Steck-Vaughn

www.HarcourtAchieve.com
1.800.531.5015

Table of Contents

Acknowledgment
Cover Illustration by Dan Clayton

ISBN 0-7398-9193-6

© 2004 Harcourt Achieve Inc.

3 4 5 6 7 8 059 11 10 09 08 07 06

Word Study Plan

1 **LOOK** at the word. _____

2 **SAY** the word. _____

3 **THINK** about each letter. _____

4 **SPELL** the word aloud. _____

5 **WRITE** the word. _____

6 **CHECK** the spelling. _____

7 **REPEAT** the steps
if you need more practice. _____

Name _____

1

Spelling Strategies

shown
shipped
shopped

pair, fair, hair

Think about the beginning sound of the word that you want to spell. Then think about a word you know that begins with the same sound.

Look for word families. The first letters of the words in a word family are different. The other letters are the same. Words in a word family rhyme.

Think about the shape of each letter in the word.

p i c k l e

If you are not sure how to spell a word, take a guess. Then look up the word in the dictionary.

Think about how a word is spelled and then write it. Try different spellings. Look at each spelling to see if it looks right.

peeceful
peaceful ✓
peacful

sub•ur•ban

Words with *un-*

unaware	unequal	unsafe	unjust
unhealthy	unlikely	unhappy	uncertain

A Circle the spelling word. Then write it on the line.
(The prefix *un* means "not.")

1. He felt (unhappy) when his team lost the game. __unhappy__

2. The ice was unsafe for skating. _____

3. Today the weather is uncertain. _____

4. The pie was divided into unequal pieces. _____

5. The person's remarks seemed unjust. _____

6. Unaware of the storm, she began hiking up the trail. _____

7. Doctors have said that smoking is unhealthy for people. _____

8. It seems unlikely that it will rain today. _____

B Circle the word that is the same as the top one.

unaware	unhealthy	unequal	unlikely	unsafe	uncertain
unawere	unhealthy	unegual	nulikely	unsefe	uncertain
unavare	nuhealthy	unequal	unlihely	nusafe	nucertain
(unaware)	unhaelthy	ueqaul	unlikely	unsafe	uncertian

C Fill in the boxes with the correct spelling words.

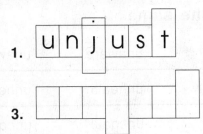

1. | u | n | j | u | s | t |

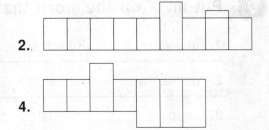

2.

3.

4.

Name _____

3

DAY
2

Words with *un-*

unaware	unequal	unsafe	unjust
unhealthy	unlikely	unhappy	uncertain

A The prefix *un* means "not." "Unhappy" means "not happy." Write the correct spelling word beside each clue.

_____ **1.** not sure, or not decided

_____ **2.** not well, or harmful

_____ **3.** not informed

_____ **4.** not probable

_____ **5.** not fair

B Find the missing letters. Then write the word.

1. __ __ s __ __ __   _____

2. u __ __ __ p __ __   _____

3. __ n __ __ t   _____

C Write the spelling words in alphabetical (ABC) order.

1. _____   **2.** _____   **3.** _____

4. _____   **5.** _____   **6.** _____

7. _____   **8.** _____

D Put an *X* on the word that is <u>not</u> the same.

1. unaware	unaware	unavare	unaware	unaware
2. unhealthy	unhealthy	unheathly	unhealthy	unhealthy
3. unequal	unequal	unequal	uneqaul	unequal
4. unlikely	unlikely	unlikely	unlikely	unlihely

Words with *un-*

unaware	unequal	unsafe	unjust
unhealthy	unlikely	unhappy	uncertain

A **Fill in each blank with a spelling word.**

1. Streets are an _____ place for children to play.

2. When her dog ran away, she felt _____.

3. He felt _____ about which show to watch.

4. She thought the umpire's ruling was _____.

5. After we made a home run, it was _____ our team would lose.

6. The classes were _____ in size.

7. Too much sugar is _____ for your body.

8. The runner was _____ that he had set a new record.

B **Fill in each blank with the correct word. (The prefix *un* means "not.")**

1. "Unsafe" means "not _____."

2. "Unequal" means "not _____."

3. "Unhappy" means "_____ happy."

4. "Unhealthy" means "not _____."

5. "Unlikely" means "_____."

6. "Uncertain" means "_____."

7. The word that means "not just" is _____.

8. The word that means "not able" is _____.

9. The word that means "not paid" is _____.

Name _____

Words with *un-*

DAY 4

unaware	unequal	unsafe	unjust
unhealthy	unlikely	unhappy	uncertain

A **Find each hidden word from the list.**

unaware	unsafe	unkind	unclear
unhealthy	unhappy	unpaid	unborn
unequal	unjust	unreserved	unswept
unlikely	uncertain	unheard	

```
a  b  u  n  a  w  a  r  e  d  u  e  f  g  u  n  c  u
s  o  n  m  e  w  h  e  r  u  n  b  o  r  n  u  e  n
u  n  h  a  p  p  y  v  e  r  r  t  h  e  r  n  a  h
n  b  e  o  w  u  s  k  i  e  e  s  a  r  e  s  b  e
u  e  a  b  i  n  r  d  u  n  s  a  f  e  s  w  f  a
u  n  l  i  k  e  l  y  n  t  e  u  n  c  l  e  a  r
n  y  t  o  v  q  e  r  k  h  r  e  r  a  i  p  n  d
p  w  h  w  h  u  y  t  i  h  v  e  n  o  h  t  w  h
a  c  y  a  n  a  t  u  n  c  e  r  t  a  i  n  i  w
i  y  t  h  e  l  n  o  d  h  d  w  u  n  p  a  i  d
u  n  e  v  e  u  n  j  u  s  t  r  m  o  r  e  q  u
```

B **Use the correct spelling words to complete the story.**

Some people think it's a lot of trouble to buy and fix healthy foods. They

are _____ of how simple it is to make tasty, wholesome meals

and snacks. What could be simpler than a fresh, ripe peach for dessert?

If we eat foods that are good for us, it's _____ we'll need

to take vitamins. A balanced diet supplies all the vitamins that a healthy

person needs.

DAY 1

Words with *non-*

nonstop	nonsmoking	nonfat	nonfiction
nonsense	nonstick	nonliving	nonbreakable

A **Fill in each blank with a spelling word. (The prefix *non* means "not.")**

1. This plastic bottle is _____.

2. He only likes to drink _____ milk.

3. Plants are living things, and rocks are _____ things.

4. We flew _____ from New York to Chicago.

5. We sat in the _____ section of the restaurant.

6. Science books were her favorite _____ books.

7. The dishes were easy to wash because of the _____ pots and pans.

8. Most words said backward sound like _____.

B **Put an X on the word that is not the same.**

1.	nonstick	nonstick	nonstick	nonstiak	nonstick
2.	nonsmoking	nonsmoking	nonsnoking	nonsmoking	nonsmoking
3.	nonsense	nonsense	nonsense	nonsense	nomsense
4.	nonliving	nonliwing	nonliving	nonliving	nonliving
5.	nonfiction	nonfiction	nonfiction	nonfictoin	nonfiction

C **Fill in each blank with the correct word. (The prefix *non* means "not.")**

1. "Nonliving" means "not _____."

2. "Nonbreakable" means "_____ breakable."

Name _____

Words with *non-*

nonstop	nonsmoking	nonfat	nonfiction
nonsense	nonstick	nonliving	nonbreakable

A Fill in the boxes with the correct spelling words.

1.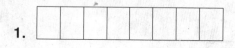

2.

3.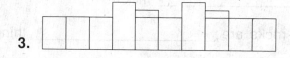

4.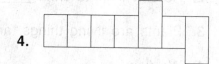

5.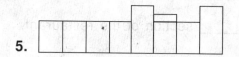

6.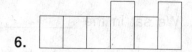

B Fill in each blank with a spelling word.

1. She worked _____ from noon until midnight.

2. That story was total _____.

3. This is one of the most popular _____ books in years.

C Answer the questions with spelling words.

1. Which words end with *ing*? _____ _____

2. Which word has four syllables? _____

D Write the spelling words in alphabetical order.

1. _____ 2. _____ 3. _____

4. _____ 5. _____ 6. _____

7. _____ 8. _____

DAY 3

Words with *non-*

nonstop	nonsmoking	nonfat	nonfiction
nonsense	nonstick	nonliving	nonbreakable

A Circle the word that is the same as the top one.

nonsense	nonsmoking	nonstick	nonliving	nonfiction	nonbreakable
nomsense	nonsmoking	nonstiek	nonlivimg	nonfietion	nonbreakalbe
nonsenes	nonsnoking	nonstick	nomliving	nonfiction	nonbreakable
nonsense	nonsmohing	nonsfick	nonliving	nonfictoin	nondreakable

B Use the correct spelling words to complete the story.

I love to fly in airplanes. You can travel fast and meet new people.

Last week I took a _____ flight to Boston. I sat

in the front section. I was next to two women. They were scientists on

their way to a meeting in Boston.

They talked to me about their work. They want to help make Earth a

clean and safe place to live. They were worried about things such as the

_____, plastic containers we use and throw away. They

said it was important to recycle as much as we could.

"It's _____ to think the problems will go away by

themselves," said one of the women. "We all need to be involved."

C Write the spelling word that comes from each root word.

break _____   smoke _____

live _____   stop _____

sense _____   stick _____

Name _____

Words with *non-*

nonstop	nonsmoking	nonfat	nonfiction
nonsense	nonstick	nonliving	nonbreakable

A Find the missing letters. Then write the word.

1. __ __ __ l __ __ __ __ __ _____

2. __ __ __ __ __ __ __ e _____

3. __ __ __ s __ __ c __ _____

4. __ __ __ __ __ t _____

B Where would you see these words? Match each spelling word with a place where the word might appear.

___d___ **1.** nonstop   **a.** on a milk carton

_____ **2.** nonsmoking   **b.** on a plastic bottle

_____ **3.** nonfat   **c.** at a library

_____ **4.** nonfiction   **d.** on an airline schedule

_____ **5.** nonbreakable   **e.** in a special area of a restaurant

C Circle the prefix in each spelling word.

nonstop   nonsense   nonsmoking   nonstick

nonfat   nonliving   nonfiction   nonbreakable

D Fill in each blank with the correct word.

1. The prefix *un* means "_____."

2. The prefix *non* means "_____."

3. "Nonstop" means "_____ stopping."

4. "Nonsense" means "_____ making sense."

Words with *pre-*

preview	pretest	preschool	prepaid
precook	prepare	preheat	prevent

A **Fill in each blank with the correct word. (The prefix *pre* means "at an earlier time" or "before.")**

1. "Prepaid" means "paid for at an _____ time."

2. "Preheat" means "to _____ at an earlier time."

3. "Preview" means "to view or look at _____."

B **Fill in each blank with a spelling word.**

1. Their daughter attends _____ classes twice a week.

2. Did you _____ the oven to 300 degrees?

3. To _____ food means to cook it just a little.

4. Before using the workbook, she took the _____.

5. We saw the _____ for the new adventure movie.

6. She will _____ for the race by running three miles every day.

7. The rain did not _____ him from leaving.

8. The hotel bill was _____ by the company.

C **Circle the word that is the same as the top one.**

preview	pretest	prepare	preschool	prepaid	prevent
prewiew	pretets	prepare	perschool	prepiad	prevemt
perview	pertest	perpare	presckool	prepaib	pervent
preveiw	pretest	preprae	preschool	predaip	prevent
preview	prestet	brepare	preschol	prepaid	prenevt

Name _____

11

DAY 2

Words with *pre-*

preview	pretest	preschool	prepaid
precook	prepare	preheat	prevent

A **Use the correct spelling words to complete the story.**

My brother cooks great pizza. It's fun to watch him. He acts like the world's greatest chef. I'm going to take my video camera to his house tonight and tape him making one of his pizzas.

We planned the taping step by step. First, my brother will

_____ the oven. Then he'll _____ a tomato

sauce and spread it on the dough. After that, he'll add cheese and other

ingredients. He'll bake the pizza for ten minutes.

After he makes the pizza, our only problem will be what to

_____ first, the tape or the pizza.

B **Fill in each blank with a spelling word.**

1. Write the words that end with the consonant *t*.

_____   _____   _____

2. Write the words that you might find in a recipe.

_____   _____   _____

3. To stop something before it happens is to _____ it.

4. To _____ means "to look at an earlier time."

C **Write the correct spelling word beside each clue.**

_____   **1.** school attended before elementary school

_____   **2.** to test before

Lesson 3

DAY 3

Words with *pre-*

preview	pretest	preschool	prepaid
precook	prepare	preheat	prevent

A **Put an *X* on the word that is <u>not</u> the same.**

1.	preview	preview	preview	preveiw	preview
2.	prevent	prevent	pervent	prevent	prevent
3.	precook	precool	precook	precook	precook
4.	pretest	pretest	pretest	pretest	prestet
5.	prepare	prepare	prepere	prepare	prepare
6.	preheat	preheat	preheat	prehaet	preheat
7.	prepaid	prepaird	prepaid	prepaid	prepaid
8.	preschool	preschool	presckool	preschool	preschool

B **Write the spelling words in alphabetical order.**

1. _____   2. _____   3. _____

4. _____   5. _____   6. _____

7. _____   8. _____

C **Circle the prefix in each spelling word.**

preview	pretest	preschool	prepare
precook	prepaid	preheat	prevent

D **Find the missing letters. Then write the word.**

1. __ __ __ __ __ __ w   _____

2. __ __ __ h __ __ __   _____

Name _____

13

DAY 4

Words with *pre-*

preview	pretest	preschool	prepaid
precook	prepare	preheat	prevent

A Use spelling words to complete the puzzle.

Across

2. to fix or get ready for

5. to keep from happening

6. nursery school

Down

1. to test before

3. to look at before

4. to cook at an earlier time

B Complete each sentence.

1. I will prepare _____.

2. I can prevent _____.

3. The preschool _____.

4. We saw a preview of _____.

5. She has prepaid _____.

14

Lesson 4 | Homonyms

DAY 1

peace	some	bow	waist
piece	sum	bough	waste

A Fill in each blank with a spelling word.

1. The two countries ended the war by signing a _____ treaty.

2. For the _____ of ten dollars, you can buy the shirt.

3. The pants were too large at the _____.

4. _____ of the students are having a bake sale to raise money.

5. I like to sit on a _____ of a tree.

6. At the end of the play, she came out to take a _____.

7. We have to be careful not to _____ our water.

8. He cut the large _____ of paper in half.

B Circle the word that is the same as the top one.

piece	peace	some	bough	waste	waist
peice	peace	sone	dough	waist	wasit
biece	paece	same	bough	wasfe	waisl
piece	peaec	soem	baugh	vaste	waste
pieec	deace	some	bougk	waste	woist
pieoe	peoce	osme	bongh	woste	waist

C Write a spelling word under each picture.

1. _____ 2. _____ 3. _____

Name _____

15

Homonyms

peace	some	bow	waist
piece	sum	bough	waste

A **Use the correct spelling words to complete the story.**

My family likes to water-ski. Last week, we took _____ friends

with us to ski at the lake. My sister wanted to ski first.

She put a life preserver around her _____ and jumped in the

lake. The boat pulled her up and she was off. Our friends cheered from the

boat when she did some of her tricks. But when my sister tried to take a

_____, she tumbled into the water. Luckily, she wasn't hurt.

B **Put an X on the word that is not the same.**

1. piece	piece	piece	peice	piece
2. peace	peaec	peace	peace	peace
3. some	some	some	some	same
4. sum	sun	sum	sum	sum
5. bow	bow	bow	bow	dow
6. bough	bough	bongh	bough	bough

C **Fill in each blank with the correct word.**

1. "Waist" and _____ are homonyms.

2. "Bow" and "bough" are _____.

3. "Peace" and _____ are homonyms.

4. "Some" and _____ are _____.

DAY 3

Homonyms

peace	some	bow	waist
piece	sum	bough	waste

A **Find each hidden word from the list.**

piece	niece	peace	waist
waste	paste	taste	baste
hum	glum	plum	sum
gum	some	come	bough
dough	row	bow	sow
mow			

```
b  t  a  s  t  e  a  b  c  w  a  i  s  t  o
a  d  y  l  u  m  h  o  e  x  l  r  o  w  p
i  o  l  p  o  g  l  u  m  u  d  o  m  l  i
s  u  l  a  y  w  e  g  u  m  l  b  e  l  e
t  g  h  s  u  m  e  h  s  o  w  a  l  w  c
u  h  l  t  o  d  o  l  n  l  y  s  i  a  g
a  p  i  e  c  e  t  s  i  s  o  t  n  s  l
u  l  i  b  o  r  t  p  e  a  c  e  a  t  m
w  u  y  o  m  y  r  e  c  l  o  o  k  e  o
o  m  o  w  e  h  u  m  e  i  n  z  u  m  b
```

B **Below are guide words. Write the spelling word that would come between each pair in the dictionary.**

_____ **1.** wage—wait

_____ **2.** stump—swim

_____ **3.** pet—pony

_____ **4.** boat—bought

_____ **5.** pace—peat

Name _____

Homonyms

peace	some	bow	waist
piece	sum	bough	waste

A Find the missing letters. Then write the word.

1. __ __ a __ __ _____

2. __ __ m __ _____

3. __ __ e __ __ _____

4. __ a __ __ e _____

B Write a paragraph using three of the spelling words.

_____

_____

_____

_____

_____

_____

C Write the correct spelling word beside each clue.

_____ **1.** a part separated from a whole

_____ **2.** found midway between knee and shoulder

_____ **3.** garbage, or careless use

_____ **4.** opposite of war

_____ **5.** branch of a tree

_____ **6.** whole amount

_____ **7.** front of a boat, or to bend at the waist

Lesson 5

Words with *dis-*

dislike	disagree	discount	disinfect
disappear	dishonest	disconnect	disorganize

A **Fill in each blank with a spelling word. (The prefix *dis* can mean "to undo.")**

1. The store offered a _____ on the sweaters after winter.

2. Do you _____ spinach?

3. You need to clean a wound to _____ it.

4. My friend and I sometimes _____ on which shows to see.

5. The magician will make the coin _____.

6. Stealing is _____.

7. His loud remarks were meant to _____ the meeting.

8. Please _____ the cord before repairing the lamp.

B **Fill in the boxes with the correct spelling words.**

1.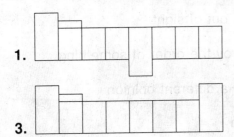

2.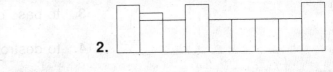

3.

4.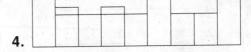

C **Circle the word that is the same as the top one.**

disappear	dishonest	discount	disconnect	disorganize
disapear	dishonest	biscount	disconect	disorganize
disappear	dishanest	disconut	disconnect	disroganize
bisappear	dishonset	discount	bisconnect	disorgamize

Name _____

Lesson 5 — Words with *dis-*

DAY 2

dislike	disagree	discount	disinfect
disappear	dishonest	disconnect	disorganize

A Write the spelling words in alphabetical order.

1. _____ 2. _____ 3. _____

4. _____ 5. _____ 6. _____

7. _____ 8. _____

B Circle the prefix in each spelling word.

dislike   disappear   disagree   dishonest

discount   disconnect   disinfect   disorganize

C Write the correct spelling word beside each clue.

_____ **1.** to subtract from a price

_____ **2.** to separate one part from another

_____ **3.** to pass out of sight

_____ **4.** to destroy the order of something

_____ **5.** to have a different opinion

_____ **6.** to clean

_____ **7.** not truthful

D Fill in each blank with a spelling word.

1. Write the words that have two syllables.

_____   _____

2. Write the word that has four syllables. _____

Words with *dis-*

dislike	**disagree**	**discount**	**disinfect**
disappear	**dishonest**	**disconnect**	**disorganize**

A **Find the missing letters. Then write the word.**

1. __ __ __ i __ __ __ __ t   _____

2. __ __ __ __ __ u __ __   _____

3. d __ __ __ p __ __ __ r   _____

4. __ __ __ a __ __ e __   _____

B **Put an X on the word that is not the same.**

1. dislike	dislike	dislike	diskile	dislike
2. disappear	disappear	disapear	disappear	disappear
3. disagree	disagree	disagree	disagree	disgree
4. dishonest	dishanest	dishonest	dishonest	dishonest
5. discount	discount	discount	disconut	discount
6. disconnect	disconect	disconnect	disconnect	disconnect
7. disinfect	disinfect	disinfect	disimfect	disinfect

C **Use the correct spelling words to complete the story.**

I _____ working with electricity. It can be dangerous. I try

to be careful when I work with plugs, wires, and outlets. This week, I fixed

an outlet in my house. I saved money by buying a new one at a _____

hardware store. I turned off the current to my house. Then I was able to

_____ the outlet and replace it with the new one, without the

fear of being shocked.

Name _____

Words with *dis-*

dislike	disagree	discount	disinfect
disappear	dishonest	disconnect	disorganize

A Find each hidden word from the list.

dislike	disable	disown
disappear	dismiss	displace
disagree	disadvantage	disbelieve
dishonest	disarm	disapprove
discount	discolor	disloyal
disconnect	discourage	disgrace
disinfect	discriminate	distrust
disorganize	disobey	discard

```
i d i s c r i m i n a t e d i
d d s d d i s a p p e a r i u
i i m i i d d i s h o n e s t
s s m s s i i e d r f d a a l
o c d a c s s l i w d i i d d
r a i b o a g n s d i s t v i
g r s l u p r e l i s c r a s
a d m e r p a d i s c o u n t
n d i s a r m i k o o l d t r
i s s p g o r s e w n o i a u
z i s n e v g o s n n r s g s
e u m m e e r b d i e g a e t
d i s b e l i e v e c a g u t
u m d i s l o y a l t n r s p
r d i s i n f e c t i n e g s
d i s p l a c e y m m e e r p
a l l w i n d i s g r a c e t
```

unaware	unsafe	nonstop	nonfat	preview
unhealthy	unhappy	nonsense	nonliving	precook
unequal	unjust	nonsmoking	nonfiction	pretest
unlikely	uncertain	nonstick	nonbreakable	preheat

A Write a spelling word under each picture.

1. _____   2. _____   3. _____

B Fill in each blank with a spelling word.

1. The sky is blue, so it seems _____ that it will rain.

2. I had to _____ the oven before baking the cookies.

3. He was _____ about his plans for the weekend.

4. Have you seen the _____ for that movie?

5. She could not understand the writing because it was _____.

6. I was working inside and _____ that it was snowing outside.

7. My family drinks _____ milk.

8. I love to read fiction and _____ stories.

9. The hurtful comments were _____.

10. They will take a _____ before they take the test.

11. I like to cook with a _____ frying pan.

12. It is _____ to eat junk food.

Name _____

preschool	peace	bow	dislike	discount
prepaid	piece	bough	disappear	disconnect
prepare	some	waist	disagree	disinfect
prevent	sum	waste	dishonest	disorganize

C **Find the missing letters. Then write the word.**

1. s _____ _____ e   _____

2. _____ o _____ _____ h   _____

3. _____ i _____ l _____ _____ e   _____

4. p _____ _____ s c _____ o ol   _____

5. d _____ _____ a _____ re _____   _____

6. d _____ _____ c _____ n n _____ ct   _____

D **Use the correct spelling words to complete the story.**

Some people like to shop for clothes, but only if they are a bargain. They

_____ for shopping by looking at ads in the newspaper. They

enjoy finding a _____ on the price of an item.

For serious shoppers, it is important to buy a quality product. They don't want

to _____ their money on something that won't last very long. To

_____ this from happening, they look carefully at each

_____ of clothing they would like to buy. The clothing must be well

made. For example, if a shirt has a button on it, the button should not be hanging

by a thread. It should be sewn on tightly. Also, a pair of pants should fit in the

_____ and the hips.

Words with *sub-*

subway	subfreezing	submarine	subsoil
subzero	suburban	subtitle	submerge

A Fill in each blank with a spelling word. (The prefix *sub* can mean "under" or "beneath.")

1. The _____ was mostly made of clay.

2. Our temperature often dips below freezing, and sometimes we have

   _____ weather.

3. The _____ slid below the water's surface.

4. The movie has a short main title and a long _____.

5. Southern Florida rarely has _____ weather.

6. We rode the _____ in Boston.

7. The _____ house looked like many others around it.

8. The boy liked to _____ his toys in the pool.

B Fill in the boxes with the correct spelling words.

1. 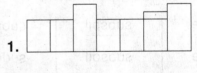   2.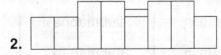

3. 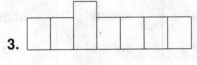   4.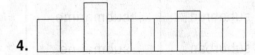

5. 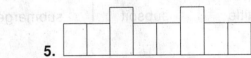   6.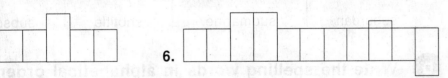

C Circle the prefix in each spelling word.

subway	subzero	subfreezing	suburban
submarine	subtitle	subsoil	submerge

Name _____

DAY
2

Words with *sub-*

subway	subfreezing	submarine	subsoil
subzero	suburban	subtitle	submerge

A Fill in each blank with the right word. (The prefix *sub* can mean "under" or "beneath.")

1. "Subfreezing" means "_____ freezing temperatures."

2. A "subtitle" is a title _____ the main title.

3. "Subsoil" is soil _____ the surface soil.

4. A "subway" is a railroad that is _____ the ground.

B Write a spelling word under each picture.

1. _____   2. _____   3. _____

C Circle the word that is the same as the top one.

suburban	submarine	subtitle	subsoil	submerge
sudurban	submanire	sudtitle	subsoil	sudmerge
subabrun	submarime	subtitle	sudsoil	submenge
suburban	submarine	subtilte	subsiol	subnerge
suburdan	sudmarine	snbtitle	subsoit	submerge

D Write the spelling words in alphabetical order.

1. _____   2. _____   3. _____

4. _____   5. _____   6. _____

7. _____   8. _____

Words with *sub-*

subway	subfreezing	submarine	subsoil
subzero	suburban	subtitle	submerge

A Write the correct spelling word beside each clue.

_____ **1.** earth that is beneath the surface

_____ **2.** to put something under water

_____ **3.** a railroad underground

_____ **4.** below 32 degrees F

_____ **5.** having to do with an area close to a city

_____ **6.** an underwater ship

B Use each spelling word in a sentence.

subway _____

suburban _____

submerge _____

submarine _____

C Put an *X* on the word that is <u>not</u> the same.

1. subway	subway	subway	sudway	subway
2. subzero	subzeno	subzero	subzero	subzero
3. suburban	suburban	suburdan	suburban	suburban
4. submarine	submanire	submarine	submarine	submarine
5. subtitle	subtitle	subtite	subtitle	subtitle
6. subsoil	subsoil	subsoil	subsoil	subsiol
7. submerge	submerge	submerge	sudmerge	submerge

Name _____

Words with *sub-*

subway	subfreezing	submarine	subsoil
subzero	suburban	subtitle	submerge

A **Use the correct spelling words to complete the story.**

Last night was the coldest it had been all winter. The weather forecast was

for temperatures well below freezing. We seldom have _____

weather where we live. I made sure we had plenty of wood for the fireplace.

We brought our cats indoors.

Our house is in a _____ part of town. It was much colder

out here than we thought it would be. It got down to two degrees below zero.

This is the first time we've had _____ temperatures.

B **Fill in each blank with a spelling word.**

1. Write the words that have two syllables.

_____   _____   _____

2. Write the words that have a long *e* sound.

_____   _____

3. Write the three-syllable word whose accent is on the last syllable.

_____

C **Find the missing letters. Then write the word.**

1. s ___ ___ ___ ___ b ___ ___   _____

2. ___ ___ ___ w ___ ___   _____

3. ___ ___ ___ m ___ ___ ___ ___ ___   _____

Words with *re-*

refill	review	repair	reclaim
recycle	refund	recharge	rewind

A Fill in each blank with a spelling word. (The prefix *re* means "to do again.")

1. You can _____ glass and newspapers, instead of throwing them away.

2. The company will _____ my money if I'm not pleased.

3. She had to _____ the car's battery.

4. The country will _____ its wetlands for use as farms.

5. My running shoes are in need of _____.

6. Will you please _____ my cup with coffee?

7. Let's _____ the tape and watch it from the beginning.

8. The class will _____ Chapter 10 before the test tomorrow.

B Circle the prefix in each spelling word.

refill	recycle	review	refund
repair	recharge	reclaim	rewind

C Find the missing letters. Then write the word.

1. ___ ___ v ___ ___ ___   _____

2. ___ ___ ___ u ___ ___   _____

D Fill in each blank with the correct word.

1. All of the spelling words, except one, have _____ syllables.

2. The word _____ has _____ syllables.

Name _____

Words with *re-*

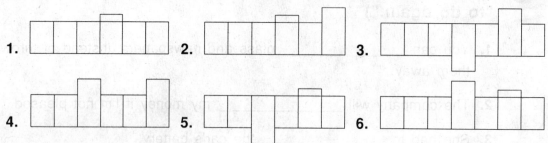

refill	review	repair	reclaim
recycle	refund	recharge	rewind

A Fill in the boxes with the correct spelling words.

1.

2.

3.

4.

5.

6.

B Circle the word that is the same as the top one.

recycle	review	repair	recharge	reclaim	rewind
recyle	reveiw	repiar	reckarge	recalim	rewimd
recycel	review	regair	rechrage	reclaim	rewinb
recycle	rewiev	repain	recharqe	reelaim	revind
necycle	reveiv	repair	recharge	reclain	rewind

C Write the spelling words in alphabetical order.

1. _____ 2. _____ 3. _____

4. _____ 5. _____ 6. _____

7. _____ 8. _____

D Complete each sentence.

1. I will <u>repair</u> _____.

2. Please <u>recycle</u> _____.

3. She has a <u>refund</u> _____.

4. Did you <u>refill</u> _____?

Words with *re-*

refill	review	repair	reclaim
recycle	refund	recharge	rewind

A **Write a paragraph using three of the spelling words.**

_____

_____

_____

_____

B **Write the correct spelling word beside each clue.**

_____ **1.** to see or examine again

_____ **2.** to recover land

_____ **3.** to wind something again

_____ **4.** to restore to new, as with a battery

_____ **5.** to fill again

_____ **6.** to treat and use again

_____ **7.** to fix a broken item

_____ **8.** money due to a person

C **Fill in each blank with the correct word.**

1. The prefix for all the spelling words is _____.

2. The prefix _____ means "to do again."

3. "Refill" means "to _____ again."

4. "Review" means "to view _____."

Name _____

31

Words with *re-*

refill	review	repair	reclaim
recycle	refund	recharge	rewind

A Put an *X* on the word that is <u>not</u> the same.

1.	refill	refill	refill	refile	refill
2.	refund	refund	refunb	refund	refund
3.	recycle	recycel	recycle	recycle	recycle
4.	repair	repair	repair	regair	repair
5.	recharge	recharge	recharge	rechorge	recharge
6.	rewind	rewind	rewind	rewind	reniwd
7.	review	reveiw	review	review	review
8.	reclaim	reclaim	recliam	reclaim	reclaim

B Use the correct spelling words to complete the story.

Let's _____ some ways that we can take care of Earth's

land, air, and water. To keep from harming our soil and streams, we can

_____ much of what we use. Paper, glass, and cans can be

saved. Old batteries and motor oil are being used again.

Instead of throwing out old clothes and broken tools, we can _____

them. Food scraps and leaves are saved as compost, which then feeds Earth.

We should think about what we do in our daily lives. It's important that we

do all we can to help our planet.

Homonyms

rain	their	haul	pair
rein	there	hall	pear

A **Fill in each blank with a spelling word.**

1. They will meet us _____ tomorrow.

2. We have an apple tree and a _____ tree in our yard.

3. Will you help your brother _____ the wood?

4. I walked down the long, wide _____.

5. He lost a _____ of gloves in the park.

6. _____ house has a beautiful garden.

7. A _____ can be used to control an animal.

8. I like the sound of _____ on a rooftop.

B **Find the missing letters. Then write the word.**

1. ___ ___ a ___   _____

2. ___ a ___ n   _____

3. ___ ___ u ___   _____

C **Fill in each blank with a spelling word.**

1. Write the word that ends with a silent *e*. _____

2. Write the two words that have five letters.

   _____   _____

3. Write the word that ends with a double consonant. _____

4. Write the word for a fruit whose first three letters spell a vegetable.

   _____

Name _____

Homonyms

rain	their	haul	pair
rein	there	hall	pear

A Circle the word that is the same as the top one.

rein	their	there	haul	pair	pear
rien	thein	tlere	haul	pain	gear
reim	thier	there	hual	pair	pean
neir	their	theer	kaul	piar	pear
rein	there	htere	haut	gair	paer

B Use the correct spelling words to complete the letter.

Dear Brenda,

   I'm having a great time at camp. _____ is a lot to do. We hike,

canoe, and learn crafts. I'm making a _____ of earrings. We eat in a

big dining _____. We haven't had any _____, so I've been

swimming every day. I wish you were here to share the fun.

                                        Your friend,

                                        Michelle

C Write the spelling words in alphabetical order.

1. _____ 2. _____ 3. _____ 4. _____

5. _____ 6. _____ 7. _____ 8. _____

D Write the spelling words that rhyme with the word pair.

1. main   train   pain   _____

2. tall   ball   fall   _____

Homonyms

rain	their	haul	pair
rein	there	hall	pear

A Write the correct spelling word beside each clue.

1. something to eat _____

2. an element of weather _____

3. to carry _____

4. a space within a building _____

5. two similar items _____

6. belonging to them _____

B Put an **X** on the word that is <u>not</u> the same.

1. their	thier	their	their	their
2. haul	haul	haul	haul	hual
3. pair	pain	pair	pair	pair
4. there	there	there	theer	there

C Write a spelling word under each picture.

1. _____   2. _____   3. _____

  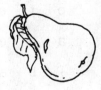

4. _____   5. _____   6. _____

Name _____

Homonyms

rain	their	haul	pair
rein	there	hall	pear

A Use each spelling word in a sentence.

rein _____

their _____

there _____

haul _____

pair _____

pear _____

hall _____

B Find each hidden word from the list.

rain	gain	main	pain
rein	their	there	haul
hall	ball	tall	mall
pair	chair	stairs	hair
pear	bear	wear	homonym

r a i h t h e r e n a h l a i
a j a o c k b b e s h a i r n
i w i m m b l e e t j u a c k
n e b o e c g a m a l l p q u
i a c n k h a r e i n j e a p
p r c y h a i k p r j u a m a
a p o m a i n v e s r t r h i
i b a l l r e c a n d l s e n
r w e a l t a l l t h e i r a

Lesson 9 · Words with *mis-*

misplace	mislead	mistreat	misfortune
misprint	misbehave	misuse	misunderstand

A Fill in each blank with a spelling word. (The prefix *mis* can mean "lack of" or "error in.")

1. I hope I didn't _____ your message.

2. Information that's untrue can be used to deceive or

   _____ people.

3. The newspaper article contained a _____.

4. To _____ an animal is cruel and unkind.

5. The young boy promised not to _____ while his parents were away.

6. _____ happened to the boy when he acted unkind.

7. We should not _____ our natural resources.

8. Did you _____ your necklace?

B Fill in the boxes with the correct spelling words.

1.

2.

3.

4.

C Circle the prefix in each spelling word.

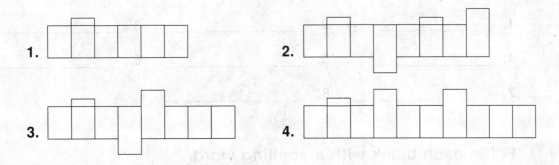

misplace   misprint   mislead   misunderstand

mistreat   misuse   misfortune   misbehave

Name _____

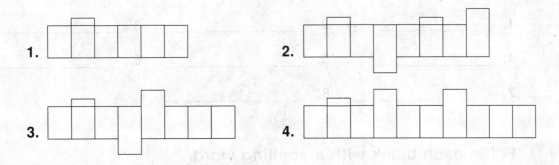

Words with *mis-*

misplace	mislead	mistreat	misfortune
misprint	misbehave	misuse	misunderstand

A Fill in each blank with a spelling word. (The prefix *mis* can mean "bad" and "badly," or "wrong" and "wrongly.")

1. Something _____ printed is a misprint.

2. "Misbehave" means "to behave _____."

3. "Mistreat" means "to treat _____."

4. "Misfortune" means "to have _____ fortune."

5. To understand wrongly is to _____.

B Find the missing letters. Then write the word.

1. ___ ___ ___ l ___ ___ ___   _____

2. m ___ ___ ___ s ___   _____

3. ___ ___ s ___ ___ a ___ e   _____

C Write the spelling words in alphabetical order.

1. _____   2. _____   3. _____

4. _____   5. _____   6. _____

7. _____   8. _____

D Fill in each blank with a spelling word.

1. Write the two words that have three syllables.

   _____   _____

2. Write the word that has four syllables. _____

Words with *mis-*

| misplace | mislead | mistreat | misfortune |
| misprint | misbehave | misuse | misunderstand |

A Put an *X* on the word that is <u>not</u> the same.

1. misplace	misplace	misplace	mispalce
2. misprint	mispirnt	misprint	misprint
3. mislead	mislead	mislaed	mislead
4. mistreat	mistreat	mistreat	mistneat
5. misuse	misuse	misnse	misuse
6. misbehave	misbehave	misbehave	misdehave
7. misfortune	mistortune	misfortune	misfortune

B Use each spelling word in a sentence.

misprint _____

mistreat _____

misunderstand _____

misplace _____

misuse _____

C Circle the word that is the same as the top one.

<u>misplace</u>	<u>misprint</u>	<u>mislead</u>	<u>mistreat</u>	<u>misuse</u>
mispalce	misprimt	mislead	misterat	misues
nisplace	misprinl	mislaed	mistreat	nisuse
misplaec	misprint	mistead	mislreat	msiuse
misplace	misgrint	nislead	mistraet	misuse

Name _____

Words with *mis-*

misplace	mislead	mistreat	misfortune
misprint	misbehave	misuse	misunderstand

A Circle the root word in each spelling word.

misplace   misprint   misunderstand   mislead

mistreat   misuse   misfortune   misbehave

B Use the correct spelling words to complete the story.

Newspaper reporters have to use care when they write stories. They

must write the facts. They can't write their opinions. And they must try not to

_____ readers.

Mistakes can happen in many different ways. Reporters might

_____ someone they interview and write the story wrong.

When the story goes to press, there could be a _____ in

the final copy. This could change the whole meaning of the piece. It's easy

to see why being a reporter is one of the hardest jobs.

C Fill in each blank with a spelling word.

1. Write the shortest and longest words.

    _____   _____

2. Write the words that end with the letter *t*.

    _____   _____

3. Write the words with the long *a* sound.

    _____   _____

Words with *con-*

contract	congregate	conform	consent
concert	concern	confide	conduct

A **Fill in each blank with a spelling word.**

1. She will _____ to be president of the club.

2. A group will _____ in the band room to practice for the parade.

3. As president, she will _____ the meeting tonight.

4. We wrote a business agreement that's called a _____.

5. Best friends often _____ in each other.

6. My main _____ is for the health of the children.

7. Shoes will _____ to the shape of your foot.

8. We attended the band _____ last week.

B **Find the missing letters. Then write the word.**

1. __ __ __ d __ __ __ 　　_____

2. __ __ n __ __ __ c t 　　_____

3. c __ __ s __ __ __ 　　_____

4. __ __ __ __ __ __ __ n 　　_____

C **Write the spelling words in alphabetical order.**

1. _____　　2. _____　　3. _____

4. _____　　5. _____　　6. _____

7. _____　　8. _____

Name _____

Lesson 10 Words with *con-*

contract	congregate	conform	consent
concert	concern	confide	conduct

A Circle the root word in each spelling word.

contraction   congregated   conformable   consenting

concerts   concerning   confided   conduction

B Write the correct spelling word beside each clue.

1. _____ to agree to something

2. _____ a musical program

3. _____ to get together

4. _____ to share a secret

C Circle the word that is the same as the top one.

contract	concert	conduct	conform	confide	consent
contarct	concent	conduet	confrom	confied	consent
contract	comcert	conbuct	conforn	confide	cansent
conlract	concert	comduct	conform	canfide	cansemt
controct	concret	conduct	contorm	confibe	consnet

D Fill in each blank with the correct word.

1. How many spelling words have two syllables? _____

2. Which spelling word has three syllables? _____

3. Which spelling words end with a silent *e*?

_____   _____

42

DAY 3

contract	congregate	conform	consent
concert	concern	confide	conduct

A Use each spelling word in a sentence.

confide _____

contract _____

concern _____

conform _____

concert _____

B Fill in the boxes with the correct spelling words.

1.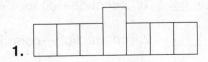

2.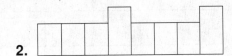

3.

4.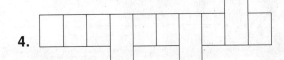

5.

6.

C Put an *X* on the word that is <u>not</u> the same.

1. contract	contract	contract	contarct	contract
2. conduct	conduct	conduct	conduct	comduct
3. consent	consent	consant	consent	consent
4. concert	concret	concert	concert	concert
5. congregate	congregate	congregate	congregate	congergate

Name _____

43

DAY 4

Words with *con-*

contract	congregate	conform	consent
concert	concern	confide	conduct

A Write the correct spelling word beside each clue.

_____ **1.** agreement

_____ **2.** to come to have the same form

_____ **3.** to lead

_____ **4.** worry

B Below are guide words. Write the spelling words that would come between each pair in the dictionary.

_____ _____ **1.** concede—condor

_____ _____ **2.** connection—contraction

_____ _____ **3.** concussion—confirm

_____ _____ **4.** conflict—connect

C Use the correct spelling words to complete the story.

Each spring, the people here _____ a "trash day." This is when we clean up our town.

Early in the morning, grownups and kids _____ with trash bags in hand. We pick up litter thrown along the roads. We find glass bottles, cans, food wrappers, and all kinds of things.

After all the trash is gathered, we sort it for things to recycle. Then we have a big picnic in the park. It's nice to live in a town where people have _____ for keeping the roadways clean.

subway	subfreezing	refill	recycle	rain
subzero	suburban	review	recharge	rein
subsoil	submarine	refund	reclaim	hall
subtitle	submerge	rewind	repair	haul

A Write a spelling word under each picture.

1. _____ 2. _____ 3. _____

B Fill in each blank with a spelling word.

1. They were going to _____ their trash to the recycling center.

2. The _____ weather kept the car from starting.

3. She lives in a _____ area outside of the city.

4. You will need to _____ that old clock several times a day.

5. You can _____ those batteries instead of buying new ones.

6. We will _____ that broken sink today.

7. It is important to _____ paper, glass, and plastic.

8. The room is at the end of the long, narrow _____.

9. Please _____ the pitcher of water when it is empty.

10. The soil beneath the surface soil is called _____.

11. When I returned the shirt, the cashier gave me a _____.

12. Can you tell me the _____ of that movie?

Name _____

misprint	misplace	contract	concert	pair
mislead	misbehave	congregate	concern	pear
mistreat	misfortune	conform	confide	there
misuse	misunderstand	conduct	consent	their

C **Find the missing letters. Then write the word.**

1. p _____ i _____   _____

2. _____ _____ _____ f i _____ e   _____

3. c _____ n _____ _____ _____ m   _____

4. _____ _____ s _____ r e _____ t   _____

5. m i _____ p _____ _____ _____ e   _____

6. c _____ n _____ _____ n _____   _____

D **Use the correct spelling words to complete the story.**

A good friend is someone who is always there for you. A friend shares your

life and is honest with you. A good friend will never _____

you. It is as though there is an unspoken agreement or _____

for trusting each other. If you are unlucky or have a _____, you

can count on a good friend to show _____ for you.

Your way of behaving or _____ is important, too. You should

always be _____ for your friend as well. When a friend wants to tell

you a secret or _____ in you, you must keep that information to

yourself. It is important for a friend to know that you can always be trusted. A

good friendship is priceless!

Words with *de-*

descend	deposit	decrease	depart
dehydrate	decide	deflate	deliver

A Fill in each blank with a spelling word. (The prefix *de* can mean "to remove," "to undo," or "to reduce.")

1. We had to _____ a stairway to get to the subway station.

2. The florist will _____ the flowers today.

3. Did you _____ your check last Friday?

4. The train will _____ for Washington at noon.

5. When you dry something, you _____ it.

6. He could not _____ where to go for his vacation.

7. You can _____ the tire by pressing the stem.

8. The hot water will cause the shirt to _____ in size.

B Fill in each blank with a spelling word.

1. Which words have three syllables?

_____ _____ _____

2. Which words have a long *i* sound?

_____ _____

3. Which word contains three *e*'s? _____

C Write a spelling word under each picture.

1. _____ 2. _____ 3. _____

Name _____

Lesson 11 Words with *de-*

DAY 2

descend	deposit	decrease	depart
dehydrate	decide	deflate	deliver

A Fill in the boxes with the correct spelling words.

1.

2.

3.

4.

5.

6.

7.

8.

B Write the spelling words in alphabetical order.

1. _____   2. _____

3. _____   4. _____

5. _____   6. _____

7. _____   8. _____

C Circle the word that is the same as the top one.

descend	dehydrate	deposit	decide	depart	deliver
decsend	dehybrate	depoist	decibe	bepart	delivre
descemd	dehydarte	degosit	decidc	depart	beliver
descenb	behydrate	deposit	decide	depamt	deliwer
descend	dehydrate	depasit	becide	pedart	deliver

48

Words with *de-*

descend	deposit	decrease	depart
dehydrate	decide	deflate	deliver

A **Fill in each blank with the correct word. (The prefix *de* can mean "undo," "remove," or "reduce." To "decode" means "to undo a code." To "defog" means "to remove fog.")**

1. "Dehydrate" means "to _____ the water."

2. "Deflate" means "to _____ the air."

B **Which spelling word might be used in discussing each topic?**

_____ **1.** clothes that shrunk in the dryer

_____ **2.** going down a rope

_____ **3.** choosing a college

_____ **4.** leaving

_____ **5.** letting air out of a bike tire

_____ **6.** adding money to an account

_____ **7.** drying fruit to preserve it

C **Use the correct spelling words to complete the story.**

When I was twelve, I wanted to go to summer camp. But my parents and

I couldn't _____ which camp to choose.

For weeks, the mail carrier would _____ information on

camps that we had asked for. At last, we chose a camp near a lake. I could

learn to canoe and water-ski there. My parents sent the camp a

_____. It was one of the best decisions we ever made.

Name _____

Words with *de-*

| descend | deposit | decrease | depart |
| dehydrate | decide | deflate | deliver |

A Find the missing letters. Then write the word.

1. __ __ p __ __ __ __ __ _____

2. __ __ p __ __ __ _____

3. d __ s __ __ __ __ _____

4. __ __ l __ __ __ __ _____

B Find each hidden word from the list.

descend   deceive   defend   dehydrate
deflate   debate   define   deposit
depart   decay   delight   decide
deliver   deduct   degree   delay
demand   decrease   decontrol

```
d  e  p  d  e  h  y  d  r  a  t  e  d  e  d
e  d  e  f  i  n  e  e  m  a  t  c  h  m  e
s  e  a  k  e  m  a  z  t  c  h  d  m  a  l
c  b  d  d  k  e  d  e  p  o  s  i  t  r  i
e  a  e  e  d  e  p  a  r  t  m  e  a  k  v
n  t  f  c  e  m  o  d  e  c  e  i  v  e
d  e  l  i  g  h  t  m  a  m  a  u  t  c  r
h  f  a  d  r  i  n  d  e  d  u  c  t  d  m
e  a  t  e  e  c  a  t  d  h  m  t  e  a  c
a  d  e  f  e  n  d  t  e  d  e  c  a  y  h
d  e  c  o  n  t  r  o  l  e  d  d  e  p  o
e  l  i  v  e  d  e  m  a  n  d  r  a  t  s
d  e  c  r  e  a  s  e  y  h  e  i  n  t  i
```

DAY 1

Homonyms

throne	shone	fair	it's
thrown	shown	fare	its

A **Fill in each blank with a spelling word.**

1. _____ beginning to rain again.

2. The bus _____ from here to the park is fifty cents.

3. The sun _____ every day at the beach.

4. The weather changed from _____ to stormy.

5. The king sat on the _____ only for ceremonies.

6. We were _____ how to play the new game.

7. She has _____ more no-hitters than any other pitcher.

8. My cat often licks _____ fur.

B **Find the missing letters. Then write the word.**

1. ___ ___ ___ n ___   _____

2. s ___ ___ ___ n   _____

C **Write a spelling word under each picture.**

1. _____   2. _____   3. _____

D **Below is a pair of guide words. Write the spelling word that would come between the pair in the dictionary.**

_____ fame—fate

Name _____

Homonyms

throne	shone	fair	it's
thrown	shown	fare	its

A Circle the root word in each spelling word.

thrown   shown   its

B Use "it's" or "its" in each sentence. ("It's" is a contraction of "it is" or "it has." "Its" is the possessive form of the pronoun "it." "Its" is used to show possession or ownership.)

1. _____ time to go to the hockey game.

2. The car was old, and _____ metal was rusted.

3. _____ been a great year for movies and music.

4. _____ a beautiful morning.

5. The tree had lost most of _____ leaves.

6. The team won many of _____ games.

7. _____ strange to have snow at this time of year.

8. Do you know if _____ too late to mail the letter?

9. Did the snake show _____ fangs?

C Circle the word that is the same as the top one.

throne	thrown	shone	fare	shown
throne	throne	shonc	faer	shown
throre	thromn	shone	fear	shone
throen	thrown	shown	fane	shomn
thnone	thorwn	shore	fare	shawn

Lesson 12

Homonyms

DAY 3

throne	shone	fair	it's
thrown	shown	fare	its

A **Use the correct spelling words to complete the story.**

There once was a story about a king who grew tired of sitting at his

_____ all day. He didn't think it was _____ to have to

stay in the castle, while others rode through the town. He called for his coach

and driver.

"_____ a splendid day for a ride," said the king to the driver.

"I'll let you wear my crown if you'll let me drive the coach." So they traded

places and had a fine ride through the town.

B **Write the correct spelling word beside each clue.**

_____ **1.** was bright

_____ **2.** a contraction

_____ **3.** tossed

_____ **4.** the official chair of a king

_____ **5.** shows ownership

_____ **6.** equal

_____ **7.** the cost of being transported, as in a bus

C **Write the spelling words in alphabetical order.**

1. _____   **2.** _____   **3.** _____

4. _____   **5.** _____   **6.** _____

7. _____   **8.** _____

Name _____

53

Homonyms

throne	shone	fair	it's
thrown	shown	fare	its

A **Use each spelling word in a sentence.**

it's _____

its _____

thrown _____

shone _____

fair _____

throne _____

shown _____

fare _____

B **Find each hidden word from the list.**

throne	shone	bone	tone
thrown	shown	grown	sown
fair	hair	chair	stair
fare	mare	stare	bare
rare	dare	hare	care

```
b o n e o g h a i r o m e s t
h c h a i r s t o n b a a t o
a m o s h o n e t r a r e a p
r o s h o w n n o g r e s n h
e s t t o n e d a r e o o e o
s t a r e o t h r o n e w w n
f a i r o c a r e w s o n e e
f a r e t h r o w n f a r n o
```

Words with -less

| harmless | careless | useless | thankless |
| painless | hopeless | helpless | thoughtless |

A Fill in each blank with a spelling word. (The suffix *less* means "lack of," "free of," "without," or "not having.")

1. He wasn't thankful to have such a _____ task.

2. The broken ax was _____ for chopping wood.

3. The rescue team did not consider the case _____.

4. When she lost her compass, the hiker felt _____.

5. The removal of the tooth was nearly _____.

6. He is never _____ with matches.

7. Her _____ comment upset her friend.

8. The garter snake is _____.

B Find the missing letters. Then write the word.

1. ___ o ___ ___ l ___ ___ ___   _____

2. ___ s ___ ___ e ___ ___   _____

3. ___ ___ l ___ l ___ s ___   _____

C Circle the word that is the same as the top one.

harmless	painless	careless	thankless	thoughtless
hanmless	gainless	careless	thamkless	thoughtless
karmless	painless	caneless	thanhless	thuoghtless
harnless	pianless	coreless	thankless	thouqhtless
harmless	paimless	carelese	thanktess	thoughttess

Name _____

DAY 2

Words with -less

harmless	careless	useless	thankless
painless	hopeless	helpless	thoughtless

A Use the correct spelling words to complete the story.

Many people are afraid of spiders. But most spiders won't hurt you at all.

They're quite _____. Some people think spiders are

_____ pests. But they eat insects that can damage plants

and vegetables. To kill every spider you see is a _____

thing to do.

If you study them closely, you'll see that spiders are beautiful and

graceful creatures.

B Fill in each blank with the correct word.

1. "Weightless" means "not having _____."

2. "Useless" means "not having _____."

3. "Blameless" means "free of _____."

4. "Painless" means "free of _____."

5. "Thankless" means "without _____."

6. "Hopeless" means "_____ hope."

7. "Thoughtless" means "without _____."

C Write the spelling words in alphabetical order.

1. _____ 2. _____ 3. _____

4. _____ 5. _____ 6. _____

7. _____ 8. _____

Words with *-less*

harmless	careless	useless	thankless
painless	hopeless	helpless	thoughtless

A Put an *X* on the word that is <u>not</u> the same.

1. helpless	helpless	helpless	helpless	heplless
2. thankless	thankless	thankless	thankless	thanhless
3. painless	painless	paimless	painless	painless
4. carless	careless	careless	careless	careless

B Use a spelling word to describe each noun.

1. a _____ job (no appreciation shown)

2. a _____ puppy (needs to be cared for)

3. a _____ spider (can't injure people)

4. a _____ operation (doesn't hurt)

5. a _____ problem (seems as though it will never be solved)

6. a _____ smoker (starts a forest fire)

7. a _____ act (not being kind)

C Fill in each blank with a spelling word.

1. Write the word that begins with a vowel. _____

2. Write the words that have a silent *e*.

_____ _____ _____

3. Write the word with the greatest number of letters. _____

4. Write the word whose root word is "thank." _____

Name _____

Words with *-less*

harmless	**careless**	**useless**	**thankless**
painless	**hopeless**	**helpless**	**thoughtless**

A Circle the suffix in each spelling word.

harmless	painless	careless	hopeless
thankless	helpless	useless	thoughtless

B Use spelling words to complete the puzzle.

Across

3. impossible

5. without care

6. having little or no worth, or not effective

Down

1. unkind

2. unable to manage by oneself

4. without pain

Words with -*ful*

thoughtful	beautiful	careful	hopeful
peaceful	harmful	truthful	thankful

A **Fill in each blank with a spelling word. (The suffix *ful* means "full of" or "having the qualities of.")**

1. She was _____ her story would win a prize.

2. My mother often tells me to be _____ when I mow the lawn.

3. His cat was a _____ gray Persian.

4. The ocean was calm and _____.

5. I'm _____ for my family and friends.

6. How _____ of you to bring me flowers!

7. Too much sun can be _____ to a person's skin.

8. He is always _____ about his feelings.

B **Write the root word of each spelling word.**

1. thoughtful _____   2. truthful _____

3. peaceful _____   4. hopeful _____

5. beautiful _____   6. thankful _____

C **Circle the word that is the same as the top one.**

careful	harmful	beautiful	thoughtful	thankful
caneful	harnful	beuatiful	thougthful	thamkful
coreful	hanmful	beautiful	thoughful	thankful
careful	harmfut	beautyful	thoughtful	thanhful
carefull	harmful	deautiful	thonghtful	thonkful

Name _____

Lesson 14

Words with -*ful*

DAY 2

thoughtful	beautiful	careful	hopeful
peaceful	harmful	truthful	thankful

A **Fill in each blank with the correct word.**

1. "Peaceful" means "full of _____."

2. "Harmful" means "full of _____."

3. "Hopeful" means "full of _____."

4. "Beautiful" means "_____ _____ beauty."

5. "Thoughtful" means "_____ _____ thought."

6. "Careful" means "full _____ _____."

7. "Thankful" means "_____ _____ _____."

8. "Truthful" means "having the qualities of _____."

B **Fill in the boxes with the correct spelling words.**

1. 2.

3. 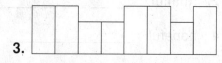 4.

5. 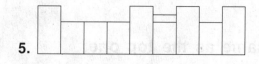 6.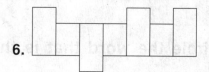

C **Complete each sentence with a spelling word.**

1. The opposite of careless is _____.

2. The opposite of dishonest is _____.

3. The opposite of thoughtless is _____.

Lesson 14

DAY
3

Words with *-ful*

thoughtful	beautiful	careful	hopeful
peaceful	harmful	truthful	thankful

A Write the spelling words in alphabetical order.

1. _____ 2. _____ 3. _____

4. _____ 5. _____ 6. _____

7. _____ 8. _____

B Find the missing letters. Then write the word.

1. __ r __ __ h __ __ __   _____

2. t __ __ __ __ __ h __ __ l   _____

3. __ __ p __ __ __ l   _____

4. __ __ r e __ __ __   _____

C Use a spelling word to describe each noun.

1. a _____ beach (when it's completely calm)

2. a _____ candidate (who thinks he can win)

3. _____ sun rays (that can damage your skin)

4. a _____ mountain climber (who watches his step)

5. _____ people (whose homes were saved from a flood)

6. a _____ sunset (that everyone stopped to admire)

D Fill in each blank with the correct word.

1. How many syllables do seven of the spelling words have? _____

2. Which spelling word has three syllables? _____

Name _____

61

Lesson 14   Words with *-ful*

thoughtful	beautiful	careful	hopeful
peaceful	harmful	truthful	thankful

A   Use each spelling word in a sentence.

thoughtful _____

peaceful _____

harmful   _____

thankful _____

truthful   _____

B   Below are guide words. Write the spelling word that would come between each pair in the dictionary.

1. _____ between—desk

2. _____ happy—human

3. _____ opened—quiet

4. _____ that—thunder

C   Use the correct spelling words to complete the story.

    I love spending summer vacations at our beach house by the sea. The

sunrise there is such a _____ sight. The bright sky and

gentle breeze coax me outside.

    I'm _____ not to stay in the sun too long. Its rays can

be _____ to my skin. But it's hard not to stay at the beach

all day. The ocean is so calm and _____. When I'm at the

beach, my troubles melt away.

Words with -*ness*

slowness	coldness	fairness	blackness
sickness	darkness	kindness	loudness

A **Fill in each blank with a spelling word.**

1. The _____ of the cat reminds me of a dark night.

2. Because of the stereo's _____, we could not talk.

3. I could never repay your _____.

4. He missed the game due to _____.

5. We have to say, in all _____, that the other team

   was good.

6. After the sun went down, _____ fell upon the campsite.

7. The train's _____ caused us to be late.

8. I will remember the _____ of that winter for a long time.

B **Find the missing letters. Then write the word.**

1. ___ ___ o ___ ___ e ___ ___   _____

2. ___ ___ u ___ n ___ ___ ___   _____

3. c ___ ___ d ___ ___ ___ ___   _____

C **Circle the word that is the same as the top one.**

sickness	darkness	fairness	kindness	blackness
sichness	barkness	fainress	kimdness	blachness
sickmess	dankness	fairness	kinbness	blockness
sickness	darkness	tairness	hindness	blackmess
siekness	darhness	foirness	kindness	blackness

Name _____

Words with -*ness*

slowness	coldness	fairness	blackness
sickness	darkness	kindness	loudness

A Circle the suffix in each spelling word.

slowness	coldness	fairness	loudness
sickness	darkness	kindness	blackness

B Which spelling word might be used in discussing each topic?

_____ 1. an umpire of a baseball game

_____ 2. a patient in a hospital

_____ 3. a band at a concert

_____ 4. a generous friend

_____ 5. a scary night

_____ 6. a turtle race

_____ 7. a freezer

C Fill in each blank with a spelling word.

1. The opposite of "warmth" is _____.

2. Flu is one kind of _____.

3. Warmhearted, helpful, and thoughtful describe the state

   of _____.

4. The word whose root word is a color is _____.

5. Which words are the opposite of "speed" and "quiet"?

   _____   _____

Lesson 15

Words with *-ness*

slowness	coldness	fairness	blackness
sickness	darkness	kindness	loudness

A Fill in the *first* blank with the correct word. Then fill in the *second* blank with the spelling word that contains the word in the *first* blank.

1. The opposite of "high" is "_____." _____

2. The opposite of "white" is "_____." _____

3. The opposite of "out" is "_____." _____

4. Oxygen is in the _____. _____

5. The opposite of "young" is "_____." _____

B Fill in the boxes with the correct spelling words.

1.    2.

3.    4.

5.   6.

7. 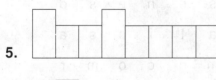   8.

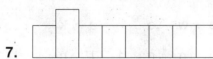

C Write the spelling words in alphabetical order.

1. _____   2. _____   3. _____

4. _____   5. _____   6. _____

7. _____   8. _____

Name _____

Words with -*ness*

slowness	coldness	fairness	blackness
sickness	darkness	kindness	loudness

A **Use the correct spelling words to complete the poem.**

In the black _____ of night, I can barely see

A mysterious ship that beckons to me.

It sails with such _____, hardly moving at all,

Riding dark waves that rise and fall.

The sails are lowered; the ship glides away.

Was it real or a dream? I don't think I could say.

B **Find each hidden word from the list.**

slowness	kindness	sameness
sickness	blackness	quietness
coldness	loudness	lightness
darkness	fairness	wetness

```
n  e  q  u  i  e  t  n  e  s  s  n  e  s  d
b  l  a  c  k  n  e  s  s  a  l  i  c  s  a
l  i  w  f  a  i  r  f  n  m  o  c  o  m  r
o  g  e  s  l  o  w  a  e  e  w  e  l  a  k
u  h  t  w  e  t  n  i  s  n  n  n  d  l  n
d  t  n  d  a  r  k  r  s  e  e  e  n  l  e
n  n  e  k  i  n  d  n  e  s  s  h  e  n  s
e  e  s  l  o  w  n  e  s  s  e  n  s  e  s
s  s  s  a  m  e  n  s  e  n  e  e  s  s  e
s  s  i  c  k  n  e  s  s  b  l  s  a  c  k
```

depart	descend	hopeful	peaceful	fair
decide	decrease	careful	beautiful	fare
deflate	deliver	truthful	thoughtful	it's
deposit	dehydrate	harmful	thankful	its

A Write a spelling word under each picture.

1. _____   2. _____   3. _____

B Fill in each blank with a spelling word.

1. The dog licked _____ sore paw.

2. I am _____ that I will pass the test.

3. Your body may _____ if you don't drink enough fluids.

4. We had to _____ a very steep stairway at her house.

5. I'm _____ my sister is my best friend.

6. How much is the bus _____ to Washington?

7. I have to _____ if I'm leaving today or tomorrow.

8. Please be _____ if you are going to drive in the rain.

9. You should always be _____ about how you feel.

10. The train will _____ at six o'clock.

11. A bad sunburn is _____ to a person's skin.

12. My bicycle tire is beginning to _____ because I ran over a nail.

Name _____

useless	careless	sickness	slowness	thrown
harmless	hopeless	coldness	fairness	throne
painless	thankless	darkness	kindness	shown
helpless	thoughtless	loudness	blackness	shone

C **Find the missing letters. Then write the word.**

1. _____ i n _____ _____ e _____ s   _____

2. p a _____ _____ l _____ _____ s   _____

3. t _____ _____ _____ _____ n   _____

4. s _____ _____ _____ e   _____

5. c o _____ _____ n e _____ _____   _____

6. _____ a r _____ l _____ _____ s   _____

D **Use the correct spelling words to complete the story.**

My parents did not want a puppy. My brother and I tried to talk them into

getting one, but it was _____. We had not _____

them that we could take care of a _____ animal.

Then one day we stopped at an animal shelter. The sound of the barking

dogs made it hard to think! Trying to pick one puppy seemed _____

because they were all so cute. But the look on one dog's face and the

_____ of her fur helped us to decide once and for all. We said we

would care for her in _____ and in health. Then my parents said we

could keep her!

Homonyms

plain	past	forth	stake
plane	passed	fourth	steak

A **Fill in each blank with a spelling word.**

1. My family has lived here for the _____ five years.

2. She pounded the tent _____ with a hammer.

3. This is the _____ summer I have mowed lawns.

4. He was happy because he had _____ the spelling test.

5. The coach paced back and _____ in front of the bench.

6. At 4:00 P.M., the _____ will depart for Portland.

7. The package arrived in a _____ brown box.

8. Our Sunday dinner will be _____ and potatoes.

B **Fill in the boxes with the correct spelling words.**

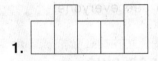

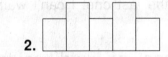

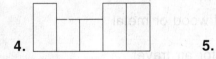

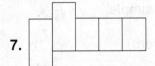

C **Write the spelling words that have a long *a* sound.**

1. _____   2. _____

3. _____   4. _____

Name _____

Homonyms

plain	past	forth	stake
plane	passed	fourth	steak

A **Find the missing letters. Then write the word.**

1. p ___ ___ s ___ ___   _____

2. ___ ___ r ___ ___   _____

3. ___ l ___ ___ e   _____

B **Use the correct spelling words to complete the story.**

Each summer, on the _____ of June, we have a family reunion.

For the _____ ten years, we've gathered at my grandparents' home.

Most of us drive to the reunion. But my cousins have to come by

_____. They live hundreds of miles away.

It's nearly time for our next reunion. I can hardly believe a year has

_____ since the last one. I can't wait to see everyone!

C **Write the correct spelling word beside each clue.**

_____   1. a piece of wood or metal

_____   2. a vehicle for air travel

_____   3. ordinary, clear, or simple

_____   4. moved on or by (verb)

_____   5. meat

_____   6. the one after third

_____   7. forward

_____   8. gone by (adjective)

Homonyms

| plain | past | forth | stake |
| plane | passed | fourth | steak |

A Write the spelling words in alphabetical order.

1. _____ 2. _____ 3. _____

4. _____ 5. _____ 6. _____

7. _____ 8. _____

B Fill in each blank with a spelling word.

1. We biked _____ the beautiful garden.

2. How do you like your _____ cooked?

3. We _____ a slow-moving car on the highway.

4. My cousin is in the _____ grade.

C Circle the word that is the same as the top one.

plain	plane	passed	fourth	forth	stake
plian	palne	pased	fourtk	fonth	stake
plaim	plane	passeb	fonrth	forth	slake
glain	plame	passcd	founth	farth	stoke
plain	plone	passed	fourth	forfh	stahe

D Write a spelling word under each picture.

 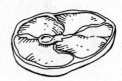

1. _____ 2. _____ 3. _____

Name _____

Lesson 16 Homonyms

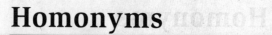

plain	past	forth	stake
plane	passed	fourth	steak

A Use each spelling word in a sentence.

plain _____

past _____

passed _____

forth _____

stake _____

fourth _____

B Find each hidden word from the list.

plain	main	grain	train	brain
plane	crane	sane	lane	vane
past	cast	fast	mast	last
stake	brake	flake	rake	make
steak	break	forth	fourth	passed

```
p  l  a  i  n  a  b  r  a  k  e  f  a  s  t
p  a  s  s  e  d  m  a  i  n  p  o  b  a  r
o  n  c  t  r  a  a  k  e  g  l  u  r  i  a
f  e  a  a  s  a  n  e  a  r  a  r  e  p  i
l  a  s  k  m  a  k  e  p  a  s  t  a  m  n
a  s  t  e  a  k  a  b  l  i  e  h  k  s  l
k  a  s  t  s  e  c  r  a  n  e  l  e  d  e
e  f  o  r  t  h  r  a  n  e  m  a  c  e  s
g  r  a  i  t  e  n  i  e  n  o  s  n  d  t
s  t  e  a  h  v  a  n  e  e  a  t  a  i  e
```

72

Words with -ly

| friendly | correctly | quickly | safely |
| honestly | partly | quietly | bravely |

A **Fill in each blank with a spelling word.**

1. To make sure you ride _____, keep your seat belt on.

2. Our _____ neighbors invited us to dinner.

3. She tiptoed _____ out of the room.

4. The man _____ risked his life to save the others.

5. The forecaster said the weather would be _____ cloudy.

6. He answered the question _____ and passed the test.

7. We _____ didn't know what to do next.

8. Let's take the short cut, to get there _____.

B **Fill in the boxes with the correct spelling words.**

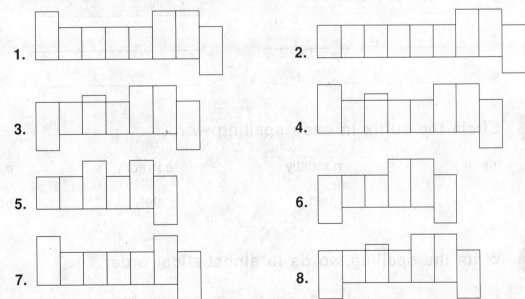

1.

2.

3.

4.

5.

6.

7.

8.

C **Write the spelling words that have three syllables.**

_____ _____ _____

Name _____

DAY 2

Words with -*ly*

friendly	correctly	quickly	safely
honestly	partly	quietly	bravely

A Fill in each blank with a spelling word.

1. Write the word that begins with a silent letter. _____

2. Write the words that have a short *e* sound.

   _____   _____

   _____   _____

3. Write the two shortest words.

   _____   _____

B Find the missing letters. Then write the word.

1. q __ __ c __ __ __   _____

2. __ __ r __ __ y   _____

3. __ __ __ e __ __ l __   _____

4. __ __ __ r __ __ t __ y   _____

C Circle the suffix in each spelling word.

friendly	honestly	correctly	partly
quickly	quietly	safely	bravely

D Write the spelling words in alphabetical order.

1. _____   2. _____   3. _____

4. _____   5. _____   6. _____

7. _____   8. _____

DAY
3

Words with -ly

friendly	correctly	quickly	safely
honestly	partly	quietly	bravely

A Write the spelling word that matches its antonym (opposite).

1. slowly _____

2. dangerously _____

3. completely _____

4. dishonestly _____

5. cowardly _____

6. unfriendly _____

B Put an *X* on the word that is <u>not</u> the same.

1. friendly	freindly	friendly	friendly	friendly
2. quietly	quietly	queitly	quietly	quietly
3. partly	party	partly	partly	partly
4. safely	safely	safely	safely	safety

C Use each spelling word in a sentence.

correctly _____

safely _____

honestly _____

quietly _____

quickly _____

bravely _____

Name _____

Words with -ly

friendly	correctly	quickly	safely
honestly	partly	quietly	bravely

A Circle the word that is the same as the top one.

friendly	honestly	quietly	correctly	bravely
freindly	homestly	guietly	cornectly	bravely
friemdly	honsetly	quielty	correctly	dravely
fniendly	honestly	quietly	correclty	bnavely
friendly	lonestly	qniety	carrectly	braevly

B Use the correct spelling words to complete the story.

My neighbor's dog had seven puppies. I chose one of them to keep.

The choice wasn't easy, though. Every one of the pups was lovable and

_____.

When the puppies saw me coming, they _____ scrambled

toward me. They cried and whined for attention.

I _____ don't know how I was able to choose just one of

the puppies.

C Complete each sentence.

1. It was <u>partly</u> _____.

2. She <u>quickly</u> _____.

3. We went <u>safely</u> _____.

4. <u>Honestly</u>, I _____.

Words with -*ment*

statement	equipment	enjoyment	encouragement
argument	payment	retirement	advertisement

A Fill in each blank with a spelling word. (The suffix *ment* indicates action or result.)

1. We need _____ for our new gym.

2. Did you see the _____ for ripe peaches?

3. Her _____ of dancing lasted many years.

4. After fifty years of work, she was ready for _____.

5. The president issued a _____ on the crisis.

6. The cheering of the crowd gave the runner great

   _____.

7. My mother settled the _____ between my sister and myself.

8. Our rent _____ is due the first day of each month.

B Find the missing letters. Then write the word.

1. e __ __ __ y __ __ __ t   _____

2. __ r __ u __ __ __ __   _____

3. __ __ t __ __ e __ __ __ __   _____

C Fill in each blank with a spelling word.

1. Write the words with two syllables.

   _____   _____

2. Write the words with four syllables.

   _____   _____

Name _____

DAY
2

Words with -ment

statement	equipment	enjoyment	encouragement
argument	payment	retirement	advertisement

A Write the spelling words in alphabetical order.

1. _____ 2. _____

3. _____ 4. _____

5. _____ 6. _____

7. _____ 8. _____

B Which spelling word might be used in discussing each topic?

_____ 1. cheering at a sports event

_____ 2. rent or telephone bill

_____ 3. furnishing a gym

_____ 4. debate

_____ 5. TV commercial

C Fill in the boxes with the correct spelling words.

1.

2.

3.

4.

5.

6.

7.

8.

Words with -*ment*

statement	equipment	enjoyment	encouragement
argument	payment	retirement	advertisement

A Find each hidden word from the list.

statement	enjoyment	environment
argument	advertisement	measurement
equipment	encouragement	employment
payment	retirement	judgment

```
j  u  a  d  v  e  r  t  i  s  e  m  e  n  t
e  q  u  i  p  m  e  n  t  o  t  o  n  p  a
n  e  h  s  t  a  t  e  m  e  n  t  j  a  s
v  i  l  l  e  n  i  o  r  t  h  y  o  y  c
i  m  e  a  s  u  r  e  m  e  n  t  y  m  a
r  a  r  g  u  m  e  n  t  r  o  y  m  e  l
o  i  n  a  u  e  m  p  l  o  y  m  e  n  t
n  j  u  d  g  m  e  n  t  n  i  t  n  t  e
m  d  s  t  a  t  n  e  s  o  f  a  t  m  e
e  r  i  c  a  w  t  o  r  l  d  g  a  l  a
n  x  y  u  n  i  v  e  r  s  e  w  h  a  t
t  e  n  c  o  u  r  a  g  e  m  e  n  t  e
```

B Use each spelling word in a sentence.

statement _____

advertisement _____

encouragement _____

equipment _____

argument _____

Name _____

Words with -ment

| statement | equipment | enjoyment | encouragement |
| argument | payment | retirement | advertisement |

A **Circle the root word in each spelling word.**

advertisement   retirement   equipment

encouragement   enjoyment   payment

B **Fill in each blank with the correct word.**

1. The suffix for all the spelling words is _____.

2. All the spelling words are _____.
   (nouns, verbs, adverbs)

3. Write the spelling words that begin with a consonant.

   _____   _____   _____

C **Use the correct spelling words to complete the story.**

If you retire at the age of sixty or so, what kinds of things will you do?
It's said that many people get the most _____ out of life
in their _____ years. They take up hobbies. They travel
from place to place. Some people go back to school.

There's an _____ on TV about volunteer work for
retirees. You work in a place, such as a hospital, for a few hours a week.
You give your time without receiving any _____. If you
plan for retirement, it can be the best time of your life.

Homonyms

doe	peer	air	bass
dough	pier	heir	base

A **Fill in each blank with a spelling word.**

1. The fawn followed the _____ into the meadow.

2. He hit the ball and ran to first _____.

3. You can _____ into this telescope.

4. A person who by law comes to own something from another person is

   called an _____.

5. The boat was tied to the _____.

6. He plays _____ guitar in a rock band.

7. The _____ at the beach smells salty.

8. He made whole wheat _____ for the bread.

B **Fill in the boxes with the correct spelling words.**

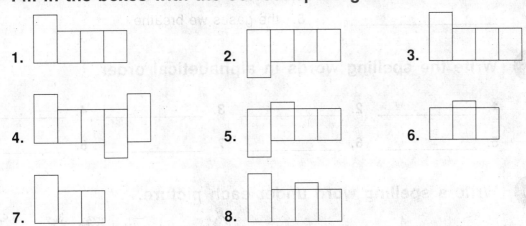

C **Which spelling word has more than one pronunciation?**

_____

Name _____

doe	peer	air	bass
dough	pier	heir	base

A   Find the missing letters. Then write the word.

1. ___ ___ i ___   _____

2. ___ o ___ ___ ___   _____

B   Write the correct spelling word beside each clue.

_____   **1.** to look at

_____   **2.** a person who inherits something

_____   **3.** bottom

_____   **4.** a singer with a deep voice

_____   **5.** a mixture of flour and water

_____   **6.** a female deer

_____   **7.** a dock

_____   **8.** the gases we breathe

C   Write the spelling words in alphabetical order.

1. _____   2. _____   3. _____   4. _____

5. _____   6. _____   7. _____   8. _____

D   Write a spelling word under each picture.

1. _____   2. _____   3. _____

82

Homonyms

doe	peer	air	bass
dough	pier	heir	base

A Use the correct spelling words to complete the story.

A man prepared for a day of sailing in his new boat. He stood on the

dock awhile to _____ at the beautiful blue sky. The shapes of the

clouds told him about the weather. The _____ around him had a

sharp bite to it, but he was dressed warmly.

He walked to the end of the _____ toward his sailboat.

He thought it would be a fine day for a sail.

B Below are guide words. Write the spelling word that would come between each pair in the dictionary.

_____ 1. pace—phone

_____ 2. doctor—done

_____ 3. basket—bath

_____ 4. heat—hire

C Put an *X* on the word that is <u>not</u> the same.

1. pier	pier	peir	pier	pier
2. dough	dough	dough	douqh	dough
3. heir	heir	heir	heir	hier
4. base	base	base	basc	base
5. air	ain	air	air	air

Name _____

Homonyms

doe	peer	air	bass
dough	pier	heir	base

A Circle the word that is the same as the top one.

dough	pier	doe	heir	bass	base
doguh	peir	boe	hier	bas	bose
bough	gier	dae	hein	boss	baes
dough	peer	doe	leir	bass	dase
daugh	pier	doc	heir	dass	base

B Write a paragraph using four of the spelling words.

_____

_____

_____

_____

_____

_____

C Fill in each blank with a spelling word.

1. The three-letter words are _____ and _____.

2. _____ ends with a double consonant.

3. Which words each contain the vowels *e* and *i*?

   _____   _____

4. _____ ends with a silent *h*.

5. The word with a double vowel is _____.

Words with -ible

possible	edible	terrible	visible
horrible	audible	incredible	sensible

A **Fill in each blank with a spelling word. (The suffix *ible* means "capable of" or "worthy of.")**

1. It's _____ to take a compass when you go for a hike.

2. Her voice was so low, it was barely _____.

3. Is it _____ that we may arrive early?

4. The acrobat performed many _____ feats.

5. That horror movie wasn't so _____.

6. Last night we had a _____ thunderstorm.

7. The mountain peak is barely _____ today.

8. Do you think that the leftover food is _____?

B **Find the missing letters. Then write the word.**

1. t __ __ __ __ b __ __   _____

2. __ o __ r __ __ __ __   _____

3. __ __ s __ __ l __   _____

4. __ __ n __ __ __ __ e   _____

C **Circle the word that is the same as the top one.**

edible	audible	possible	sensible	incredible
ebidle	aubidle	posslbile	sersible	increbible
edidle	audible	passible	sensible	incredibel
edible	audibel	possible	seusible	incerdible
edibel	andible	gossible	sensidle	incredible

Name _____

Lesson 20

DAY 2

Words with *-ible*

possible	edible	terrible	visible
horrible	audible	incredible	sensible

A Write the spelling words in alphabetical order.

1. _____ 2. _____

3. _____ 4. _____

5. _____ 6. _____

7. _____ 8. _____

B Circle the suffix in each spelling word.

possible   terrible   visible   audible

horrible   incredible   sensible   edible

C Complete each sentence with a spelling word.

1. If something can be seen, it is _____.

2. If something can be heard, it is _____.

3. If something can be eaten, it is _____.

4. If something is unbelievable, it is _____.

5. If something is capable of happening, it is _____.

6. If something makes good sense, it is _____.

D Fill in each blank with a spelling word.

1. Write the word with four syllables. _____

2. Write the words that begin with vowels.

_____ _____

Lesson 20 — Words with -*ible*

possible	edible	terrible	visible
horrible	audible	incredible	sensible

A Fill in the boxes with the correct spelling words.

1.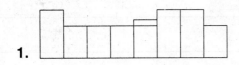

2.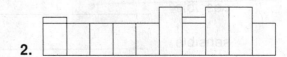

3.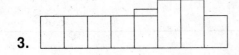

4.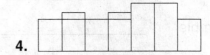

5.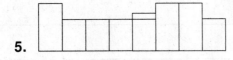

6.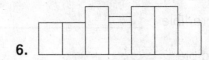

7.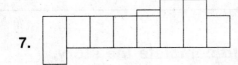

8.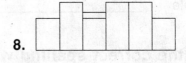

B Write the spelling word that matches its antonym (opposite).

1. believable _____

2. wonderful _____

3. inedible _____

4. not reasonable _____

5. unseen _____

C Choose a spelling word that can describe each noun.

1. _____ fire 2. _____ mushrooms

3. _____ rain 4. _____ agreement

5. _____ whistle 6. _____ rainbow

Name _____

87

Words with -ible

possible	edible	terrible	visible
horrible	audible	incredible	sensible

A Use each spelling word in a sentence.

possible _____

sensible _____

edible _____

terrible _____

visible _____

incredible _____

audible _____

horrible _____

B Use the correct spelling words to complete the story.

Hundreds of years ago, people had to travel on land for thousands of miles to get from Europe to India. Most people thought it was not

_____ to get there faster by sea. But a man named Christopher Columbus thought he could find a route to India by sea. He asked the king and queen of Spain for money for his journey.

After more than a month at sea, his crew was running out of drinking water and _____ food. Then, on October 12, 1492, what we know as the Bahama Islands became _____. He had not found India, but had discovered a world new to him.

Columbus made four trips in all to try to find a route to India. Although he never succeeded, Christopher Columbus is an important part of history.

partly	friendly	statement	payment	air
safely	honestly	encouragement	steak	heir
bravely	correctly	advertisement	base	plane
quietly	quickly	retirement	pier	bass

A **Write a spelling word under each picture.**

1. _____   **2.** _____   **3.** _____

B **Fill in each blank with a spelling word.**

1. With the _____ of friends, he was successful.

2. We walked _____ so that we would not scare the deer.

3. He made it home _____ during the snowstorm.

4. The _____ of the sculpture was made of stone.

5. She made a brave _____ to the class.

6. I am _____ responsible for what happened.

7. Who is the _____ to England's throne?

8. My cat is very sweet and _____.

9. She answered each question _____ and passed the test.

10. His car _____ is due every month.

11. The movie is about to start, so we should leave _____.

12. My grandparents are enjoying their _____.

Name _____

plain	passed	stake	edible	sensible
enjoyment	past	doe	audible	possible
argument	forth	dough	visible	horrible
equipment	fourth	peer	terrible	incredible

C **Find the missing letters. Then write the word.**

1. d o _____ _____ _____   _____

2. s _____ _____ k _____   _____

3. _____ _____ s _____   _____

4. _____ l _____ _____ _____   _____

5. p _____ _____ r   _____

6. _____ a s _____ _____ _____   _____

7. i _____ c _____ e _____ i b _____ e   _____

D **Use the correct spelling words to complete the story.**

Some people like to hear scary stories or watch horror movies. They like to

be frightened by _____ movie scenes filled with terror. Sometimes

people are terrified by something that is _____ on the screen like a

ghost. Sometimes just a sound that is barely _____ is enough to

scare them.

I don't understand how anyone can watch scary movies. If I see a scary movie,

I cover my eyes so that I can't see what is happening. I think it is much more

_____ to watch an adventure movie or one that is romantic. Then it

is _____ to have sweet dreams instead of nightmares!

Words with *-able*

likable	usable	movable	lovable
believable	returnable	valuable	breakable

A **Fill in each blank with a spelling word.**

1. The job applicant seemed _____ and experienced.

2. Save that bottle because it's _____ at the store.

3. The log was so heavy, it was barely _____.

4. Is that a nonbreakable or _____ jar?

5. His story sounded _____, but it wasn't true.

6. If you recycle paper, it's _____ more than once.

7. What a _____ puppy!

8. Gold is more _____ than silver.

B **Fill in the boxes with the correct spelling words.**

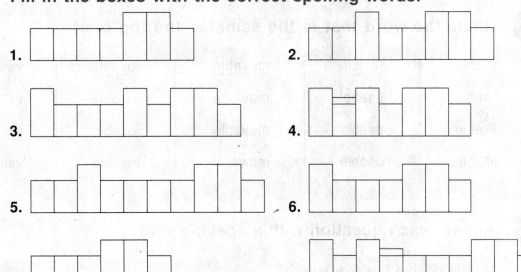

1.

2.

3.

4.

5.

6.

7.

8.

C **Write the spelling words that have four syllables.**

_____   _____   _____

Name _____

Words with -*able*

likable	usable	movable	lovable
believable	returnable	valuable	breakable

A Circle the suffix in each spelling word.

likable   believable   usable   returnable

movable   valuable   lovable   breakable

B Write the root word of each spelling word. (In each of the root words, the silent *e* was dropped before the suffix *able* was added. Example: size + able = sizable.)

1. likable _____
2. valuable _____
3. movable _____
4. usable _____
5. believable _____
6. lovable _____

C Circle the word that is the same as the top one.

likable	usable	movable	lovable	valuable
likabel	usabel	movable	lavoble	valuable
likeble	usable	movadle	lovabel	valuadle
likable	usoble	mowable	lovable	valuabel

D Answer each question with a spelling word.

1. Which word has five vowels? _____

2. Which word begins with a vowel? _____

3. Which word has a long *i* sound? _____

4. Which word has a long *a* sound? _____

Words with *-able*

likable	usable	movable	lovable
believable	returnable	valuable	breakable

A Find the missing letters. Then write the word.

1. __ e __ __ __ __ n __ __ __ e   _____

2. u __ __ __ __ __   _____

3. __ i __ a __ __ __   _____

4. m __ __ __ __ __   _____

B Put an *X* on the word that is <u>not</u> the same.

1. likable	likable	likable	lihable	likable
2. believable	believable	beleivable	believable	believable
3. usable	usable	usable	usadle	usable
4. returnable	returnable	returnable	returnable	returnoble
5. movable	movable	mowable	movable	movable
6. valuable	valuable	valuable	valauble	valuable
7. lovable	lovable	lovable	lovable	lovadle
8. breakable	braekable	breakable	breakable	breakable

C Choose a spelling word that can describe each noun.

1. _____ tools   **2.** _____ glass

3. _____ furniture   **4.** _____ story

5. _____ diamond   **6.** _____ kitten

Name _____

Words with *-able*

DAY 4

| likable | usable | movable | lovable |
| believable | returnable | valuable | breakable |

A **Use the correct spelling words to complete the story.**

I once had a teacher who asked our class to list the best things about ourselves. "Make your list _____," she said. "Make your list sound just the way you are."

Some of us didn't know what to write. She used the lesson to show us how to look for our most _____ qualities. It turned out to be a very _____ lesson.

B **Complete each sentence with a spelling word.**

1. If something can be broken, it's _____.

2. If something can be moved from one spot to another, it's

_____.

3. If something is enjoyable, it's _____.

4. If a story is worthy of belief, it's _____.

5. If something can be taken back, it's _____.

6. If something has much worth, it's _____.

C **Write the spelling words in alphabetical order.**

1. _____   **2.** _____

3. _____   **4.** _____

5. _____   **6.** _____

7. _____   **8.** _____

| patience | threw | who's | your |
| patients | through | whose | you're |

A **Fill in each blank with a spelling word.**

1. _____ going to the game with us?

2. She _____ the ball over the fence.

3. _____ going to do well today!

4. The two _____ shared a hospital room.

5. We hiked _____ the forest to the waterfall.

6. It takes _____ to do a jigsaw puzzle.

7. Do you know _____ car that is?

8. _____ mother is very thoughtful.

B **Find the missing letters. Then write the word.**

1. t ___ ___ ___ ___ ___   _____

2. ___ ___ ___ r   _____

3. ___ h ___ ' ___   _____

4. ___ ___ t ___ ___ ___ t ___   _____

C **Circle the word that is the same as the top one.**

patience	patients	through	whose	you're
pateince	patienls	throuqh	whose	yon're
patiemce	patients	thruogh	wkose	you'er
patience	gatients	thnough	whase	you're
potience	pateints	through	whoes	your'e

Name _____

DAY 2

Homonyms

patience	threw	who's	your
patients	through	whose	you're

A Write the spelling words in alphabetical order.

1. _____
2. _____
3. _____
4. _____
5. _____
6. _____
7. _____
8. _____

B Fill in each blank with the correct word.

1. "Threw" and _____ are homonyms.

2. "Whose" and _____ are homonyms.

3. "Your" and "you're" are _____.

4. "Patience" and _____ are _____.

C Fill in the blanks with "who's" or "whose." ("Who's" is a contraction of "who is" or "who has." "Whose" is used to show possession or ownership.)

1. _____ coming to our house?

2. _____ dog is the black one?

3. I know _____ going to the dance.

4. Do you know anyone _____ been to China?

5. _____ pencil is this one?

6. _____ allowed to go to the movies?

7. I'm not sure _____ car that is.

8. _____ coming over for dinner?

Lesson 22

Homonyms

patience	threw	who's	your
patients	through	whose	you're

A Fill in the boxes with the correct spelling words.

1.

2.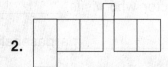

3.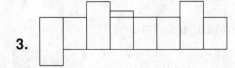

4.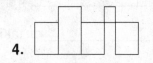

5.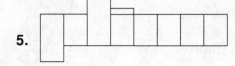

6.

7.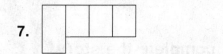

8.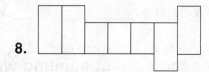

B Fill in the blanks with "you're" or "your." ("You're" is a contraction of "you are." "Your" is used to show ownership or possession.)

1. _____ horse is well trained.

2. I see _____ wearing the hat I gave you.

3. _____ supposed to watch _____ sister today.

4. Is the party at _____ house?

5. _____ doing a great job of painting the room!

6. _____ the best swimmer on our team.

7. It's time for _____ favorite TV show.

8. Have you decided what _____ going to do this summer?

Name _____

DAY 4

Homonyms

| patience | threw | who's | your |
| patients | through | whose | you're |

A Complete each phrase with a spelling word.

1. a doctor who visits _____ in their homes

2. _____ a baseball to the batter

3. drove _____ the tunnel

4. the _____ of taking one step at a time

5. too dark to see where _____ going

6. find _____ way back home

7. an idea _____ time has come

8. a person _____ willing to take a stand

B Use the correct spelling words to complete the story.

You're a great baseball player. _____ pitching arm is very

strong; you once _____ three no-hitters in a row. You have

a lot of _____ with new players, teaching them how to improve

their ball game. _____ better at bat than you? Not many can hit

as well as you. For a player _____ career in baseball is just

beginning, _____ terrific!

C Fill in each blank with the correct word.

1. _____ is a contraction of "you are."

2. "Who's" is a _____ of "who is" or "who has."

3. The words _____ and _____ show ownership.

Words with *-tion*

caution	education	affection	transportation
direction	protection	operation	construction

A Fill in each blank with a spelling word. (The suffix *tion* means "action involved with.")

1. The best _____ here is the subway.

2. The _____ to repair his shoulder was successful.

3. A well-rounded _____ connects you to the world.

4. Do you know from what _____ the wind is blowing?

5. _____ has begun on the new house.

6. I show a lot of _____ to my cat.

7. Drivers should use _____ on icy roads.

8. I wear a hat outdoors for _____ from the sun.

B Write the spelling words in alphabetical order.

1. _____ 2. _____

3. _____ 4. _____

5. _____ 6. _____

7. _____ 8. _____

C Fill in each blank with a spelling word.

1. Write the words that have five vowels.

_____ _____ _____

2. Write the words that have four syllables.

_____ _____ _____

Name _____

Words with *-tion*

caution	education	affection	transportation
direction	protection	operation	construction

A **Use the correct spelling words to complete the story.**

Our state government is responsible for doing many things. The

_____ of people from place to place is a big concern of

the state. The state plans the _____ of new roads. It

has to help build schools for the _____ of its citizens.

And its people need _____ from crime.

Running a state government is very complex. People with different

talents must communicate and work together for its smooth

_____.

B **Find the missing letters. Then write the word.**

1. __ __ r __ __ __ i __ __   _____

2. __ f __ __ __ t __ __ __   _____

3. __ __ u __ __ __ n   _____

C **Which spelling word might be used in discussing each topic?**

_____ 1. building a tower

_____ 2. surgery

_____ 3. planes, trains, and cars

_____ 4. umbrellas and raincoats

_____ 5. schools and universities

Lesson 23

Words with *-tion*

caution	education	affection	transportation
direction	protection	operation	construction

A **Use each spelling word in a sentence.**

caution _____

protection _____

affection _____

direction _____

B **Write the spelling word that matches its antonym (opposite).**

1. destruction _____

2. dislike _____

3. ignorance _____

4. recklessness _____

C **Write a spelling word under each picture.**

1. _____ 2. _____ 3. _____

D **Fill in each blank with the correct word.**

1. "Transport" is the root word of _____.

2. _____ is the root word of "protection."

3. "Operate" is the root word of _____.

4. _____ is the root word of "education."

Name _____

101

Words with *-tion*

| caution | education | affection | transportation |
| direction | protection | operation | construction |

A Use spelling words to complete the puzzle.

Across

2. taking care of something
4. being careful
5. bicycles, cars, ships, and trains
8. the act of directing

Down

1. the act of building
3. instruction
6. a fond or tender feeling
7. a process, or the act of working

Words with *-sion*

invasion	decision	vision	erosion
confusion	television	explosion	collision

A Fill in each blank with a spelling word.

1. An _____ of termites weakened the wood.

2. The lack of ground cover caused the soil's _____.

3. She made the _____ to study abroad.

4. The earthquake caused the _____ of the gas tanks.

5. When the traffic lights broke, there was _____ among the drivers.

6. The _____ of the waiters caused their trays to spill.

7. I need glasses to correct my _____.

8. The play was shown on _____ last night.

B Find the missing letters. Then write the word.

1. ___ r ___ ___ ___ n _____

2. ___ ___ c ___ ___ ___ o ___ _____

3. c ___ ___ ___ u ___ ___ ___ _____

4. ___ n ___ ___ s ___ ___ ___ _____

C Write a spelling word under each picture.

1. _____ 2. _____ 3. _____

Name _____

Lesson 24   Words with -*sion*

invasion	decision	vision	erosion
confusion	television	explosion	collision

A Fill in the boxes with the correct spelling words.

1.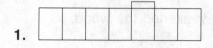

2.

3.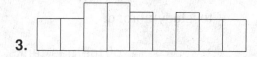

4.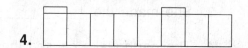

5.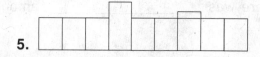

6.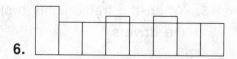

B Write the correct spelling word beside each clue.

_____ **1.** crash

_____ **2.** wearing away

_____ **3.** sight

_____ **4.** entrance by force

_____ **5.** the process of deciding

_____ **6.** disorder

_____ **7.** a form of entertainment

_____ **8.** a violent release of energy

C Answer each question with a spelling word.

1. Which spelling word appears in another spelling word?

_____

2. Which word does it appear in? _____

Lesson 24

Words with *-sion*

invasion	decision	vision	erosion
confusion	television	explosion	collision

A **Find each hidden word from the list.**

invasion	vision	division
confusion	explosion	transfusion
decision	erosion	conclusion
television	collision	provision

```
i t r a n s f u s i o n x p x
n e x p l o s i o n f x d r i
v l x d t e c o n f u s i o n
d e c i s i o n t e s l v v v
a v a v a s l c v h i e i i a
v i s i o n l l s i o n s s s
i s i s c i i u s i n o o i i
s i o i d e s s i n c l u o o
i o n o n s i i d i v i s n n
o n e n o c o n c l u s i o n
e r o s i o n n p r o v i s i
```

B **Fill in each blank with a spelling word.**

1. The root word of this spelling word is "decide." _____

2. The root word of this spelling word is "erode." _____

3. The root word of this spelling word is "confuse." _____

4. The root word of this spelling word is "collide." _____

5. Write the word that has four syllables. _____

6. Write the word that has two syllables. _____

Name _____

Words with -*sion*

invasion	decision	vision	erosion
confusion	television	explosion	collision

A Write the spelling words in alphabetical order.

1. _____   2. _____   3. _____

4. _____   5. _____   6. _____

7. _____   8. _____

B Which spelling word might be used in discussing each topic?

_____ **1.** a wreck

_____ **2.** eyeglasses

_____ **3.** dynamite

_____ **4.** commercials

_____ **5.** war

_____ **6.** loss of topsoil

_____ **7.** which candidate to vote for

C Use the correct spelling words to complete the story.

With the invention of _____, the events of the world are

there for us to see. We can share the wonders of life within and beyond our

planet without leaving our homes. We've seen the _____ of

an atom bomb on TV. We watched astronauts play golf on the moon. We

saw the Berlin Wall come down. We've seen hurricanes and floods and their

aftermath. For better or worse, TV has changed our _____

of the world.

Lesson 25

DAY 1

Words with *-sion*

expansion	mission	extension	possession
permission	tension	admission	comprehension

A **Fill in each blank with a spelling word.**

1. The math problem was beyond his _____.

2. We need an _____ cord for this lamp.

3. An _____ ticket to the concert costs a lot of money.

4. The rancher gave us _____ to swim in her pond.

5. He had twenty-three marbles in his _____.

6. They built an _____ bridge across the river.

7. The _____ of the group was to create peace.

8. His headache was a result of _____.

B **Find the missing letters. Then write the word.**

1. ___ e ___ ___ ___ o ___   _____

2. ___ ___ s s ___ ___ ___   _____

3. e ___ ___ a ___ ___ ___ ___ ___   _____

C **Put an *X* on the word that is not the same.**

1. permission	permission	permission	permision
2. extension	extemsion	extension	extension
3. possession	possession	possessoion	possession
4. comprehension	comprehension	comprehension	comperhension
5. expansion	expansion	expansion	expamsion
6. admission	admission	admission	abmission

Name _____

Words with *-sion*

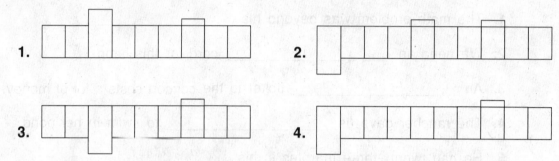
A Fill in the boxes with the correct spelling words.

1.

2.

3.

4.

5.

6.

B Below are guide words. Write the spelling word that would come between each pair in the dictionary.

_____ **1.** expenditure—extract

_____ **2.** exit—expend

_____ **3.** permit—post

_____ **4.** advertise—decision

_____ **5.** possible—terrible

C Write the correct spelling word beside each clue.

_____ **1.** ownership

_____ **2.** growth

_____ **3.** entrance

_____ **4.** understanding

Words with -*sion*

expansion	mission	extension	possession
permission	tension	admission	comprehension

A **Fill in each blank with a spelling word.**

_____ 1. Add *ex* to this word, and you have another spelling word.

_____ 2. Add *ad* to this word, and you have another spelling word.

_____ 3. You might see this word on a ticket to a ball game.

_____ 4. This word can describe an extra electrical cord.

_____ 5. This word has two sets of the same double consonants.

_____ 6. This word has four syllables.

B **Write the spelling words in alphabetical order.**

1. _____ 2. _____ 3. _____

4. _____ 5. _____ 6. _____

7. _____ 8. _____

C **Circle the word that is the same as the top one.**

expansion	tension	mission	possession	comprehension
expamsion	tensiom	nission	possession	comprehensiom
exgansion	temsion	mision	posession	conprehension
expansion	tension	mission	possessiom	comperhension
expansoin	tensoin	missiom	possessoin	comprehension

Name _____

Words with -*sion*

expansion	mission	extension	possession
permission	tension	admission	comprehension

A **Use the correct spelling words to complete the story.**

Our town is growing fast. Most of the _____ is north of town. Companies have asked for _____ from the city to build offices there. This has caused a lot of _____ between those who live in the north part of town and the companies. Homeowners don't want more buildings. And they don't want more traffic near their homes. So they've asked the city to take _____ of much of the land. They want to have a park built so growth won't get out of control.

B **Complete each sentence with spelling words.**

1. "Comprehend" is the root word of _____.

2. "Expand" is the root word of _____.

3. "Permit" is the root word of _____.

4. "Admit" is the root word of _____.

5. _____ and _____ are two-syllable words.

C **Use each spelling word in a sentence.**

admission _____

tension _____

mission _____

extension _____

possession _____

threw	caution	education	vision	confusion
through	direction	transportation	invasion	television
patience	operation	construction	decision	explosion
patients	affection	protection	erosion	collision

A Write a spelling word under each picture.

1. _____ 2. _____ 3. _____

B Fill in each blank with a spelling word.

1. Which _____ is the wind blowing?

2. It is important to study and get a good _____ .

3. Please walk up the stairs and _____ those doors.

4. His grandfather taught him _____ and kindness.

5. She bought a new pair of glasses to correct her _____ .

6. The cabin provided _____ from the snowstorm.

7. My little sister sometimes throws _____ to the wind.

8. They are planning the _____ of the new school.

9. The doctor has to take care of many _____ .

10. She _____ the football across the field to her friend.

11. He made the _____ to attend the play.

12. The constant rain caused the _____ of this soil.

Name _____

likable	believable	who's	mission	expansion
usable	returnable	whose	tension	possession
movable	breakable	your	extension	permission
lovable	valuable	you're	admission	comprehension

C **Find the missing letters. Then write the word.**

1. w _____ _____ s _____   _____

2. _____ i _____ s _____ _____ n   _____

3. _____ om _____ r e _____ ension   _____

4. _____ i _____ a _____ _____ e   _____

5. _____ o _____ _____   _____

6. p _____ r _____ iss _____ on   _____

D **Use the correct spelling words to complete the story.**

I like to hear my grandmother tell stories. I can listen to her for hours.

Once she told me a remarkable but _____ tale that happened

during the Great Depression. Most people at that time were poor and had little to

eat. One day someone came to my grandmother's door and asked for something

to eat. Food was very _____ at that time, but she decided to give

him some. She gave him soup in a _____ dish. The dish was so

hot that he dropped it! Of course, the dish was no longer _____.

But he promised to work to repay her for her kindness. My grandmother was

so impressed with what he had done that she asked him to stay. One year later

she married him!

Homonyms

| coarse | idol | vain | flee |
| course | idle | vein | flea |

A **Fill in each blank with a spelling word.**

1. We tried in _____ to get tickets to the concert.

2. Of _____ we will go to the soccer game.

3. The vest was made of _____ fabric.

4. I hope that wasn't a _____ on my dog.

5. His _____ is Martin Luther King, Jr.

6. I'd like to go to the beach and be _____ for a while.

7. The animals were able to _____ from the wildfire.

8. Do you know the difference between a _____ and an artery?

B **Fill in the boxes with the correct spelling words.**

1.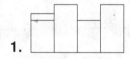

2.

3.

4.

5.

6.

7.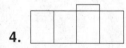

8.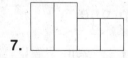

C **Complete each sentence.**

1. My <u>idol</u> is _____ because _____.

2. The <u>coarse</u> _____.

Name _____

Homonyms

coarse	idol	vain	flee
course	idle	vein	flea

A Find the missing letters. Then write the word.

1. ___ ___ ___ a   _____

2. ___ ___ l ___   _____

3. ___ a ___ ___   _____

4. ___ ___ u ___ ___ ___   _____

B Write the correct spelling word beside each clue.

_____ 1. blood vessel

_____ 2. inactive

_____ 3. insect

_____ 4. route

_____ 5. run away

_____ 6. rough

_____ 7. one that is adored

_____ 8. very proud

C Circle the word that is the same as the top one.

coarse	course	idol	idle	vein	vain
coanse	cuorse	ibol	idel	veim	voin
coares	coures	idal	ible	vien	vain
coarse	course	idol	idle	vein	vian
caorse	conrse	idot	idlc	wein	vaim

Homonyms

coarse	idol	vain	flee
course	idle	vein	flea

A **Use the correct spelling words to complete the story.**

My dog Boy is eleven years old. He doesn't run around as often as he used

to. The _____ hair around his muzzle is turning gray.

Cats used to _____ when he was outside. Now they fearlessly

walk through our yard, while he sits _____ on the front porch. Not

even a pesky _____ bothers him anymore.

I'll always love old Boy. And he's still my best friend.

B **Fill in each blank with the correct word.**

1. "Vain" and _____ are homonyms.

2. "Flee" and _____ are pronounced the same.

3. _____ and _____ have two syllables.

4. "Coarse" and _____ are pronounced the same.

5. "Coarse" and "course" are _____.

6. A _____ for "idle" is _____.

7. "Vein" and _____ are _____.

C **Write the spelling words in alphabetical order.**

1. _____ 2. _____ 3. _____

4. _____ 5. _____ 6. _____

7. _____ 8. _____

Name _____

Homonyms

coarse	idol	vain	flee
course	idle	vein	flea

A **Use each spelling word in a sentence.**

course _____

idle _____

flee _____

vain _____

B **Put an _X_ on the word that is <u>not</u> the same.**

1.	coarse	coarse	coarse	course	coarse
2.	vain	vane	vain	vain	vain
3.	course	course	course	course	cource
4.	idol	idol	idal	idol	idol

C **Complete each phrase with a spelling word.**

1. _____ cloth

2. to _____ the country

3. a teenage _____

4. a _____ collar

5. _____ time

6. a _____ in the arm

7. a _____ attempt

8. an obstacle _____

9. _____ manners

Words with *-ence*

| confidence | violence | conference | independence |
| experience | difference | coincidence | competence |

A Fill in each blank with a spelling word.

1. We met in New Orleans by _____.

2. Many people believe there's too much _____ on TV.

3. Her _____ in herself helped her get the job.

4. Winning a gold medal is an _____ she'll never forget.

5. The United States declared its _____ from England in 1776.

6. I attended a _____ on writing for magazines.

7. What's the _____ between butter and margarine?

8. The committee questioned his _____ to do the job.

B Put an *X* on the word that is <u>not</u> the same.

1. confidence	confidence	confidemce	confidence
2. experience	experience	experience	expereince
3. violence	voilence	violence	violence
4. competence	competence	conpetence	competence
5. independence	independence	independence	independbence

C Write the spelling words in alphabetical order.

1. _____ 2. _____ 3. _____

4. _____ 5. _____ 6. _____

7. _____ 8. _____

Name _____

Lesson 27

DAY 2

Words with -ence

confidence	violence	conference	independence
experience	difference	coincidence	competence

A Find the missing letters. Then write the word.

1. ___ ___ o ___ ___ n ___ ___   _____

2. ___ ___ p ___ ___ i ___ ___ e   _____

3. ___ i ___ ___ ___ r ___ ___ c ___   _____

4. c ___ ___ ___ c ___ ___ ___ n c ___   _____

B Write the correct spelling word beside each clue.

_____ **1.** the state of being competent

_____ **2.** the opposite of dependence

_____ **3.** a meeting for discussion

_____ **4.** feeling certain

_____ **5.** two things that happen at the same time by accident

_____ **6.** the state of being different

_____ **7.** brutal action

C Complete each sentence with spelling words.

1. The three words with four syllables are _____,

    _____, and _____.

2. _____ has a double consonant.

3. The first four letters of these words are the same:

    _____ and _____.

Words with -*ence*

confidence	violence	conference	independence
experience	difference	coincidence	competence

A Find each hidden word from the list.

confidence   independence   consequence
experience   difference   competence
violence   conference   coincidence

```
d  c  o  i  n  c  i  d  e  n  c  e  p  i  d
c  o  m  p  e  t  e  n  c  e  x  x  d  n  o
i  n  d  e  p  e  n  d  e  n  c  e  i  d  n
e  s  c  o  i  n  c  i  d  e  n  c  f  e  f
x  e  x  p  e  r  i  e  n  c  e  e  f  p  a
p  q  c  o  n  v  i  o  l  e  n  c  e  e  r
e  u  i  n  d  e  p  e  n  d  e  n  r  c  e
r  e  e  c  o  n  f  i  d  e  n  c  e  d  n
i  n  c  o  n  f  e  r  e  n  c  e  n  n  e
e  c  o  n  s  e  q  u  e  n  c  e  c  n  e
n  k  c  e  c  o  m  p  e  t  e  n  e  c  t
```

B Write the root word of each spelling word.

1. confidence _____   **2.** competence _____

3. conference _____   **4.** difference _____

C Fill in each blank.

1. Each spelling word ends with the letters _____.

2. Which spelling words can stand alone without the ending "ence"?

_____   _____

Name _____

Words with -ence

| confidence | violence | conference | independence |
| experience | difference | coincidence | competence |

A Use the correct spelling words to complete the story.

Some students get summer jobs to earn extra money. From this

_____, there's much they can learn. They may bag

groceries, cook food, or cut people's grass. Doing their jobs well will give

them greater _____. They'll learn to take pride in their

work. Being responsible for doing a job is a big step toward

_____.

B Complete each sentence.

1. I have the most <u>confidence</u> when I _____

   _____.

2. When I see <u>violence</u>, _____.

3. Our <u>conference</u> was _____.

4. <u>Independence</u> is _____

   _____.

5. My <u>experience</u> taught me _____

   _____.

6. My greatest <u>competence</u> is _____.

7. The <u>difference</u> between _____

   _____.

8. It was a <u>coincidence</u> that _____

   _____.

Words with -ance

| attendance | finance | endurance | appearance |
| admittance | entrance | ambulance | performance |

A **Fill in each blank with a spelling word.**

1. Our chorus gave a great _____ last night.

2. _____ at the football game reached a record high.

3. The _____ to the garden was filled with lovely plants.

4. A marathon is a test of _____.

5. The sign on the door said "No _____."

6. The _____ arrived at the scene of the accident.

7. A person's _____ is very important when interviewing for a job.

8. The secretary of _____ manages the money.

B **Fill in the boxes with the correct spelling words.**

1.

2.

3.

4.

5.

6.

7.

8.

C **How many spelling words begin with vowels?** _____

Name _____

Lesson 28 — Words with -*ance*

DAY 2

| attendance | finance | endurance | appearance |
| admittance | entrance | ambulance | performance |

A Write the root word of each spelling word.

1. attendance _____   2. entrance _____

3. admittance _____   4. endurance _____

5. performance _____   6. appearance _____

B Put an *X* on the word that is <u>not</u> the same.

1. ambulance	ambulance	anbulance	ambulance
2. performance	performance	performance	preformance
3. entrance	entarnce	entrance	entrance

C Write the correct spelling word beside each clue.

_____ 1. money matters

_____ 2. the power to withstand hardship

_____ 3. a vehicle for taking people to the hospital

_____ 4. something that appears

_____ 5. the act of attending

_____ 6. a play or concert

_____ 7. permission to enter

_____ 8. the opposite of exit

D Write the spelling words that have double consonants.

_____   _____

Words with *-ance*

attendance	finance	endurance	appearance
admittance	entrance	ambulance	performance

A Find the missing letters. Then write the word.

1. __ e __ f __ __ m __ __ __ e _____

2. __ __ n __ n __ __ _____

3. a __ __ __ l __ __ c __ _____

4. __ __ t __ __ d __ __ c __ _____

B Circle the word that is the same as the top one.

admittance	endurance	entrance	appearance	performance
admittance	endunance	entramce	appeanance	perfromance
abmittance	enburance	entrance	appaerance	pertormance
admitance	enduranec	enlrance	apearance	performance
admittamce	endurance	entnarce	appearance	performamce

C Fill in each blank with a spelling word.

_____ 1. If you take away the first two letters, the remaining word means "a dazed state."

_____ 2. This word has the name of a fruit in it.

_____ 3. This word has a number in it.

_____ 4. This word has the name of something worn by baseball catchers.

_____ 5. If you rearrange the letters in this word, you get the words "can" and "fine."

_____ 6. The words "for man" are in this word.

Name _____

DAY 4

Words with -ance

attendance	finance	endurance	appearance
admittance	entrance	ambulance	performance

A Write the spelling words in alphabetical order.

1. _____   2. _____   3. _____

4. _____   5. _____   6. _____

7. _____   8. _____

B Use the correct spelling words to complete the story.

Last night, I saw a _____ of one of my favorite rock

bands. To gain _____ to the concert, I had to have a

special badge. I received the badge when I bought my ticket.

The band made its _____ on the stage at nine o'clock.

They sounded great. Over ten thousand fans were in _____.

It was a night I'll never forget.

C Below are guide words. Write the spelling word that would
come between each pair in the dictionary.

_____   **1.** appoint—attic

_____   **2.** advice—annual

_____   **3.** enter—enhance

_____   **4.** exit—future

D Write the shortest and the longest spelling words.

_____   _____

DAY 1

Words with -*y*

company	mystery	library	country
factory	apology	enemy	biology

A **Fill in each blank with a spelling word.**

1. The equipment is assembled at the _____.

2. _____ is the study of life.

3. I hope you'll accept my _____.

4. We expected our _____ to arrive about 6 o'clock.

5. Our _____ has some interesting books about animals.

6. The _____ of the missing diamond has never been solved.

7. The hawk is an _____ of the mouse.

8. We've traveled outside our own _____ many times.

B **Find the missing letters. Then write the word.**

1. c ___ m ___ ___ ___ y   _____

2. ___ p ___ ___ ___ ___ ___   _____

3. ___ ___ ___ t ___ r ___   _____

C **Complete each sentence with spelling words.**

1. _____ and _____ have a long *i* sound.

2. _____ and _____ begin with vowels.

3. The word with the fewest number of syllables is _____.

4. The two words that rhyme are _____ and _____.

5. The two words beginning with the same letter are _____ and

   _____.

Name _____

Words with -*y*

company	mystery	library	country
factory	apology	enemy	biology

A Put an *X* on the word that is <u>not</u> the same.

1. company	company	company	conpany	company
2. factory	factony	factory	factory	factory
3. mystery	mystery	mystrey	mystery	mystery
4. apology	apology	apology	apology	apotogy
5. library	lidrary	library	library	library
6. enemy	enemy	enemy	ememy	enemy
7. country	country	conutry	country	country
8. biology	biology	biology	diology	biology

B Use each spelling word in a sentence.

factory _____

mystery _____

country _____

library _____

C Fill in each blank with a spelling word.

_____ **1.** The word "log" is found in these two words.

_____

_____ **2.** The word "my" is found in these two words.

_____

_____ **3.** The word "try" is found in this word.

Lesson 29

Words with -*y*

company	mystery	library	country
factory	apology	enemy	biology

A **Use the correct spelling words to complete the story.**

My friends and I visited a small _____ that makes stuffed

animals. They make bears, dogs, monkeys, and rabbits. We went to the

_____ to watch them piece together the parts of each animal.

We asked the people at the factory how they keep track of which parts go

where. They told us it's no _____. They work on the same animals

on the same day. That way there's no chance of putting a bear's head on a

dog's body. We learned a lot at the factory that day.

B **Which spelling word might be used in discussing each topic?**

_____ **1.** overdue books

_____ **2.** an opponent in war

_____ **3.** guests in the home

_____ **4.** wrongdoing

_____ **5.** patriotism

_____ **6.** studying plants and animals

_____ **7.** a manufacturing plant

_____ **8.** something unexplained

C **Write the spelling words that have four syllables.**

_____ _____

Name _____

Words with *-y*

company	mystery	library	country
factory	apology	enemy	biology

A Find each hidden word from the list.

company	country	county	berry
factory	biology	lady	gypsy
mystery	geometry	story	ruby
apology	chimney	pulley	army
library	journey	valley	ferry
enemy	diary	dairy	sentry

```
h  r  o  u  v  n  c  r  s  x  e  i  m  s  u
s  e  n  t  g  e  o  m  e  t  r  y  a  c  c
e  n  e  m  y  j  o  d  a  i  r  y  e  b  o
n  e  v  a  p  o  l  o  g  y  m  y  s  e  m
t  h  e  o  s  u  c  h  i  m  n  e  t  r  p
r  l  a  d  y  r  f  o  d  e  f  v  s  r  a
y  c  h  i  m  n  e  y  h  d  c  a  t  y  n
o  m  y  s  t  e  r  y  b  i  o  l  o  g  y
p  u  l  l  e  y  r  e  n  a  u  l  r  o  r
f  a  c  t  o  r  y  h  i  r  n  e  y  j  u
e  n  e  c  o  u  n  t  r  y  t  y  k  l  b
b  i  o  l  l  i  b  r  a  r  y  a  r  m  y
g  s  m  o  y  l  e  f  r  s  m  x  d  c  h
```

B Write the spelling words in alphabetical order.

1. _____   2. _____   3. _____

4. _____   5. _____   6. _____

7. _____   8. _____

Lesson 30 — Homonyms

principal	guest	aloud	presence
principle	guessed	allowed	presents

A **Fill in each blank with a spelling word.**

1. He was admired as a man of _____.

2. No one was _____ to swim in the lake before the month of May.

3. I _____ it would take five hours to drive to the beach.

4. Her favorite _____ were the wristwatch and the trip to the city on the train.

5. She recited the poem _____ to herself.

6. I was a _____ at their house for three days.

7. The _____ of our school is very nice.

8. Her _____ was felt in the room.

B **Fill in the boxes with the correct spelling words.**

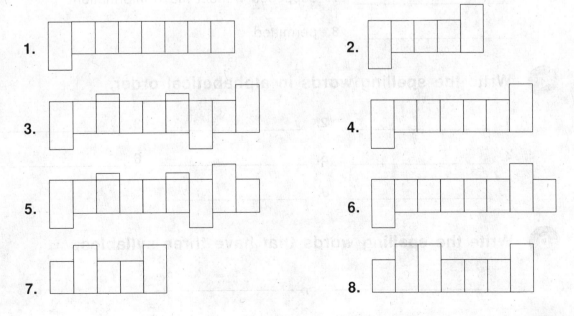

Name _____

Lesson 30 Homonyms

DAY 2

principal	guest	aloud	presence
principle	guessed	allowed	presents

A Write a spelling word under each picture.

1. _____   2. _____   3. _____

B Write the correct spelling word beside each clue.

_____ 1. louder than a whisper

_____ 2. visitor

_____ 3. a basic truth or law

_____ 4. the condition of being present

_____ 5. gifts

_____ 6. a person with authority

_____ 7. supposed without much information

_____ 8. permitted

C Write the spelling words in alphabetical order.

1. _____   2. _____   3. _____

4. _____   5. _____   6. _____

7. _____   8. _____

D Write the spelling words that have three syllables.

_____   _____

Lesson 30

Homonyms

principal	guest	aloud	presence
principle	guessed	allowed	presents

A **Find the missing letters. Then write the word.**

1. g ___ ___ ___ ___ e ___   _____

2. p ___ ___ n ___ ___ ___ l ___   _____

3. ___ r ___ ___ ___ ___ c ___   _____

4. ___ ___ l ___ ___ ___ d   _____

B **Below are guide words. Write the spelling word that would come between each pair in the dictionary.**

_____ 1. alone—alphabet

_____ 2. gone—guessing

_____ 3. prepare—presented

_____ 4. prime—principals

C **Fill in each blank with a spelling word.**

1. _____ is a plural word.

2. The words with double consonants are _____ and

_____

3. The words that can mean a person are _____ and

_____.

4. Write the words that come from these root words.

guess _____   allow _____

present _____

Name _____

Homonyms

| principal | guest | aloud | presence |
| principle | guessed | allowed | presents |

A **Use each spelling word in a sentence.**

principal _____

aloud _____

allowed _____

presence _____

guest _____

B **Circle the word that is the same as the top one.**

principle	guessed	allowed	presents	presence
prinicple	guesseb	allawed	presemts	presents
prinicical	geussed	allowed	persents	presemce
pirnciple	guessed	alouwed	presents	presnece
primciple	quessed	alloued	presnets	presence
principle	guesesd	alloweb	bresents	persence

C **Use the correct spelling words to complete the story.**

You've reached the end of this book. By now you know that the main

_____ of good spelling is to practice each day.

Could you have _____, many weeks ago, that you would

know how to spell so many words? Learning to spell correctly and to write

well are like _____ that no one else can give you. You give

them to yourself by working hard and always using what you've learned.

attendance	finance	flee	company	library
admittance	entrance	flea	factory	enemy
endurance	appearance	vain	mystery	guest
ambulance	performance	vein	apology	principal

A **Write a spelling word under each picture.**

1. _____ 2. _____ 3. _____

B **Fill in each blank with a spelling word.**

1. I offered an _____ to her because I was wrong.

2. The large _____ at the theater on opening night was more

   than we expected.

3. We searched in _____ for our lost cat.

4. I enjoy the _____ of good friends.

5. Does your uncle work at that _____?

6. What is in outer space is a _____ to many people.

7. It takes _____ to work twelve hours a day.

8. The singer will make an _____ on Saturday night.

9. Her _____ at the show was the best I had ever seen.

10. The forest fire caused the animals to _____.

11. I need to return these books to the public _____.

Name _____

violence	experience	idol	biology	country
conference	difference	idle	principle	guessed
competence	coincidence	coarse	presents	aloud
confidence	independence	course	presence	allowed

C **Find the missing letters. Then write the word.**

1. _____ i _____ l _____ _____ _____   _____

2. _____ u e _____ _____ _____ d   _____

3. _____ o u _____ _____ e   _____

4. _____ i f _____ e r _____ _____ c e   _____

5. p _____ _____ s e _____ c e   _____

6. i n d _____ _____ e n _____ e n c e   _____

D **Use the correct spelling words to complete the story.**

My cousin is trying out a new career. He wants to be a teacher. Though he

lacks _____ in this new field, he has _____ in himself.

He believes he will gain _____ and succeed.

His guiding _____ has always been "never say never." He

repeats this and several other sayings _____ to himself every day.

It may be a _____, but he has always been very successful in

everything he does. He has many friends, and most people like to be in his

_____. I think he will make a great teacher!

My Word List

Words I Can Spell

Put a ✓ in the box beside each word you spell correctly on your weekly test.

1

- ☐ unaware
- ☐ unhealthy
- ☐ unequal
- ☐ unlikely
- ☐ unsafe
- ☐ unhappy
- ☐ unjust
- ☐ uncertain

2

- ☐ nonstop
- ☐ nonsense
- ☐ nonsmoking
- ☐ nonstick
- ☐ nonfat
- ☐ nonliving
- ☐ nonfiction
- ☐ nonbreakable

3

- ☐ preview
- ☐ precook
- ☐ pretest
- ☐ prepare
- ☐ preschool
- ☐ preheat
- ☐ prepaid
- ☐ prevent

4

- ☐ peace
- ☐ piece
- ☐ some
- ☐ sum
- ☐ bow
- ☐ bough
- ☐ waist
- ☐ waste

5

- ☐ dislike
- ☐ disappear
- ☐ disagree
- ☐ dishonest
- ☐ discount
- ☐ disconnect
- ☐ disinfect
- ☐ disorganize

Words To Review

If you miss a word on your test, write it here. Practice it until you can spell it correctly. Then check the box beside the word.

_____
_____
_____
_____
_____
_____
_____
_____
_____
_____
_____
_____
_____
_____
_____
_____
_____

Name _____

Words I Can Spell

Put a ✓ in the box beside each word you spell correctly on your weekly test.

6

- ☐ subway
- ☐ submarine
- ☐ subzero
- ☐ subtitle
- ☐ subfreezing
- ☐ subsoil
- ☐ suburban
- ☐ submerge

7

- ☐ refill
- ☐ repair
- ☐ recycle
- ☐ recharge
- ☐ review
- ☐ reclaim
- ☐ refund
- ☐ rewind

8

- ☐ rain
- ☐ haul
- ☐ rein
- ☐ hall
- ☐ their
- ☐ pair
- ☐ there
- ☐ pear

9

- ☐ misplace
- ☐ mistreat
- ☐ misprint
- ☐ misuse
- ☐ mislead
- ☐ misfortune
- ☐ misbehave
- ☐ misunderstand

10

- ☐ contract
- ☐ conform
- ☐ concert
- ☐ confide
- ☐ congregate
- ☐ consent
- ☐ concern
- ☐ conduct

Words To Review

If you miss a word on your test, write it here. Practice it until you can spell it correctly. Then check the box beside the word.

_____

_____

_____

_____

_____

_____

_____

_____

_____

_____

_____

_____

_____

_____

_____

_____

_____

My Word List

Words I Can Spell

Put a ✓ in the box beside each word you spell correctly on your weekly test.

11

- [ ] descend
- [ ] dehydrate
- [ ] deposit
- [ ] decide
- [ ] decrease
- [ ] deflate
- [ ] depart
- [ ] deliver

12

- [ ] throne
- [ ] thrown
- [ ] shone
- [ ] shown
- [ ] fair
- [ ] fare
- [ ] it's
- [ ] its

13

- [ ] harmless
- [ ] painless
- [ ] careless
- [ ] hopeless
- [ ] useless
- [ ] helpless
- [ ] thankless
- [ ] thoughtless

14

- [ ] thoughtful
- [ ] peaceful
- [ ] beautiful
- [ ] harmful
- [ ] careful
- [ ] truthful
- [ ] hopeful
- [ ] thankful

15

- [ ] slowness
- [ ] sickness
- [ ] coldness
- [ ] darkness
- [ ] fairness
- [ ] kindness
- [ ] blackness
- [ ] loudness

Words To Review

If you miss a word on your test, write it here. Practice it until you can spell it correctly. Then check the box beside the word.

_____
_____
_____
_____
_____
_____
_____
_____
_____
_____
_____
_____
_____
_____
_____
_____
_____
_____

Name _____

Words I Can Spell

Put a ✓ in the box beside each word you spell correctly on your weekly test.

Words To Review

If you miss a word on your test, write it here. Practice it until you can spell it correctly. Then check the box beside the word.

16

- ☐ plain
- ☐ plane
- ☐ past
- ☐ passed
- ☐ forth
- ☐ fourth
- ☐ stake
- ☐ steak

17

- ☐ friendly
- ☐ honestly
- ☐ correctly
- ☐ partly
- ☐ quickly
- ☐ quietly
- ☐ safely
- ☐ bravely

18

- ☐ statement
- ☐ argument
- ☐ equipment
- ☐ payment
- ☐ enjoyment
- ☐ retirement
- ☐ encouragement
- ☐ advertisement

19

- ☐ doe
- ☐ dough
- ☐ peer
- ☐ pier
- ☐ air
- ☐ heir
- ☐ bass
- ☐ base

20

- ☐ possible
- ☐ horrible
- ☐ edible
- ☐ audible
- ☐ terrible
- ☐ incredible
- ☐ visible
- ☐ sensible

My Word List

Words I Can Spell

Put a ✓ in the box beside each word you spell correctly on your weekly test.

21

☐ likable   ☐ movable

☐ believable   ☐ valuable

☐ usable   ☐ lovable

☐ returnable   ☐ breakable

22

☐ patience   ☐ who's

☐ patients   ☐ whose

☐ threw   ☐ your

☐ through   ☐ you're

23

☐ caution   ☐ affection

☐ direction   ☐ operation

☐ education   ☐ transportation

☐ protection   ☐ construction

24

☐ invasion   ☐ vision

☐ confusion   ☐ explosion

☐ decision   ☐ erosion

☐ television   ☐ collision

25

☐ expansion   ☐ extension

☐ permission   ☐ admission

☐ mission   ☐ possession

☐ tension   ☐ comprehension

Words To Review

If you miss a word on your test, write it here. Practice it until you can spell it correctly. Then check the box beside the word.

_____

_____

_____

_____

_____

_____

_____

_____

_____

_____

_____

_____

_____

_____

_____

_____

Name _____

My Word List

Words I Can Spell

Put a ✓ in the box beside each word you spell correctly on your weekly test.

Words To Review

If you miss a word on your test, write it here. Practice it until you can spell it correctly. Then check the box beside the word.

Word Study Sheet

(Make a check mark after each step.)

Name _____

Words	1 Look at the Word	2 Say the Word	3 Think About Each Letter	4 Spell the Word Aloud	5 Write the Word	6 Check the Spelling	7 Repeat Steps (if needed)

141

Graph Your Progress

Number of words correctly spelled:

(Color or shade in the boxes.)

	Lesson 1	Lesson 2	Lesson 3	Lesson 4	Lesson 5	Lesson 6	Lesson 7	Lesson 8	Lesson 9	Lesson 10	Lesson 11	Lesson 12	Lesson 13	Lesson 14	Lesson 15	Lesson 16	Lesson 17	Lesson 18	Lesson 19	Lesson 20	Lesson 21	Lesson 22	Lesson 23	Lesson 24	Lesson 25	Lesson 26	Lesson 27	Lesson 28	Lesson 29	Lesson 30
8																														
7																														
6																														
5																														
4																														
3																														
2																														
1																														

Name _____